BUSINESS

PROCRASTINATOR

*The Lessons I Have Learnt, Developed, and Taught
and Should Have Followed*

GAVEN FERGUSON

bp

www.thebusinessprocrastinator.com

Gaven Ferguson

First printed in the United States of America
First Edition 2021
First Printing 2021
Second Printing 2025

ISBN: 978-0-646-82632-5

10 9 8 7 6 5 4 3 2 1

Thanks for purchasing my book. If you enjoyed the read, I'd love to hear your honest opinion.

After 30 years

Finally, the book I should have written (and then read)

Table of Contents

INTRODUCTION

I will assume a few things in this book as you read, and I will write to you as if the following are already underway. So, you have your idea, you've done the leg work, and you've carried out a bit of research. You found something or see something — some idea or gap that no one has tapped into yet and you think that there is a business there. You have discussed the idea with someone who may think differently than you and has no vested interest in the potential business. This person is often called a mentor, and they are worth their weight in gold. Trust me.

Now, I want you to STOP. Stop, sit back, and look at the idea. Look at the research you have done and the results you have obtained. I want you to ask yourself these five simple questions before you do anything else:

1. Are you ready to put in 100% effort? Are you willing to do whatever it takes (legally) to achieve what you want?
2. Do you really, in your heart and soul, think that this idea is meeting an unmet need?

3. Can you focus long enough on the goal ahead
    — do you have FOCUS FOCUS FOCUS?
4. Are you ready to step to the edge of the cliff
    and risk it all?
5. What is your goal? What specifically do you
    want to achieve? Be honest with yourself.

If you answer "no" to any of them or hesitate on one or more, then sit back and ask yourself why you are hesitant. Answering these questions right now may just save you more than you can imagine.

If you answer "yes" to every one of these questions with complete confidence and zero hesitation, then let's get cracking…

Some of you may be asking who I am or what makes me an expert on this topic. I do not really see myself as an expert but rather as an everyday guy who has been around a few years and has seen a few things. I find that practical experience and knowledge are key parts of being able to learn. Without them, you are just a bookworm who dreams big. As Richard Stewart says, "Basic business knowledge will enable you to assess the professional advice you receive, and to question it if necessary."

I do not profess to know what you are going through, and just like Robin Williams tells Matt Damon in the movie *Good Will Hunting*, "You think I know the first thing about how hard your life has been, how you feel, who you are, because I read Oliver Twist?" I don't. I want to understand, and I want to help, which is why I decided to write this book.

As Robin Williams said, "I'm fascinated. I'm in." And so should you be. But if you are not willing to listen to people who have already made mistakes and been at the cliff's edge, then don't complain if you make a mistake and it doesn't work the way you wanted. It's going to happen, so get ready for it.

I didn't have an overly difficult life growing up. My dad was a police officer, and my mum worked in a pharmacy for most of her life. We had cars and a nice house with a big backyard. I got my first job when I was 12, sweeping the floor of a signwriter's shop in Berwick, Victoria. After 18 months, I managed to secure a new job at a local butcher's. I hated that job, but I loved what I learned. You see, butchers don't beat around the bush. I have come to realize that anyone wielding a knife and cutting up dead flesh usually tells it to you straight.

I remember my childhood primary school fondly. It was a great little Primary School called Hallem Valley Primary. It was a wonderful community with only 36 kids, and I remember walking down the dusty road or catching the bus to get there. I remember seeing some new classrooms coming in on big trucks. They were the first movable buildings I had ever seen, and I was impressed. I would walk to school week after week, wondering if there were any more buildings coming or some new and exciting construction happening.

I have always loved to watch things being built, so when the bridge next to the school collapsed one day while we were on the bus, I was in heaven. I would go down to the fence in the following days and watch as they repaired it. It was great to see the big trucks and cranes creating a new and impressive concrete structure. I think I got this from my mum, who told me stories about watching the road workers in her village near Birmingham repairing old Roman roads.

I grew up with good grades, but nothing suggested that I would be a mega-star or an amazing sportsman. I wasn't into sports much. I leaned towards the nerdier things of life, like computers and board games, but I was still into Rock and Roll. I still love adventures and computers today and often find myself sidetracked in search of some interesting tidbit of information or location.

I am not rich financially speaking, and while I have dreamt about it many times, I can honestly say I am happy with how my life is. I love what I do, and I enjoy what I create.

A real passion of mine is to see a project become successful, which has allowed me to experience many aspects of the business world in a variety of different industries. American film actress Alice Barker once said, "I used to often say to myself, I am being paid to do something that I enjoy doing, and I would do it for free, because it just felt so good doing it." I sometimes feel the same way, even today.

I came across a list many years ago that has always stuck with me. I know that the list is pretty straightforward, but I like it none the less. It sort of sums up a bit of what I am trying to say in the book. Benjamin Franklin's 12 Time Management Lessons are simple and straight to the point, and I refer to them a few times throughout. Given the nature of the book, I had to throw them in somewhere.

1. Strive to be Authentic - be honest with yourself
2. Favour Trusting Relationships
3. Always maintain a lifestyle that will maximise your energy
4. Always listen to your biorhythms and organise your plan accordingly
5. Set few priorities and stick with them
6. Turn things down that are not consistent with your priorities
7. Set aside time for focused effort
8. Constantly look for ways of doing things faster and better
9. Learn to build solid processes than run without attention
10. Learn to spot troubles ahead and find solutions
11. Break your goals into smaller units and handle one tasks at a time
12. Finish what's important and stop doing what's not worthwhile.

Mr Franklin gets it, and many of the principles of his list are in this book in one way or another. It's like I was channelling him when I was writing. Probably because I have had this list for a long time.

I have had my fair share of personal opportunities and experiences, and I think I can honestly say I have learnt a thing or two from them. Yet somewhere along the way, I seem to lose sight of more of them than I would like to. I am a Procrastinator. That's right: I AM A PROCRASTINATOR. Man, does it feel good to finally get it out there and feel the burden lifted! I waste time so much sometimes that if I just knuckled down, I would be far more successful.

"Time is really the only capital that any human being has, and the only thing he can't afford to lose."

Thomas Edison

You will not find me flashing around how many people I have helped to succeed or how much money I have. You will not see me driving a luxury car or sitting in a big, flashy office (though I have had my share of nice offices). These are good, but they only show you results, which is exactly how social media is used these days: they are often fake results, or at the very least, manipulated results so that you can get sucked into buying a course from someone.

This sort of advertising is simply a way to show off and try to get into your head. It's about making you wish you had something and then confusing you just enough so that the person doing it needs to show you the light at the end of the tunnel. Someone will eventually get rich from the advice they give, but I doubt it will be you.

Rubbing it in your face is not my style. I think that wealth and happiness come in other ways as well. Being happy and stable in life is often what people want, and the rest is just smoke and mirrors. But that smoke and mirrors are often intertwined with some amazing insights and lessons from which you should learn. I know I did.

Now, I'm sure some of those people will say it's because I do not have it and that they are entitled to their opinion. But please understand where I am coming from. I don't help people build businesses just to drive fancy cars or flash my money around. I do it because I love it.

It is that simple.

So, for now, let me share with you some lessons I have learnt from a variety of examples I have heard, seen, and experienced about starting and running a business.

But before we begin, let's discuss what procrastination is, its causes, and what it may cost you.

The Root Cause of Procrastination

Why is it that, as human beings, we often behave in ways that we do not really want to? How often have you said or done something only to later cringe at the thought of it? The truth is that your behaviour is mostly driven by your unconscious mind, especially behaviours that are hard to explain from an intellectual point of view. Procrastination is knowing what to do, having the ability and desire to do it, but still not doing it. Although there are many apparent causes for procrastination, the root cause for this illogical behaviour resides in your unconscious mind.

Your conscious mind is limited in its ability to deal with life. What you have conscious control over is mostly limited to one thing at a time, which is why using your willpower to create any real change rarely works long-term. What you need to do is to change the automatic behaviour that resides in your unconscious mind—that part of you that controls all the vital functions of your mind and body. You can try to overcome procrastination by using willpower, but it will usually be a short-term change. The cause for procrastination is not your conscious actions but your unconscious associations that are, to a large extent, responsible for your behaviour.

Your nervous system is designed to preserve you, so when fear presents itself to your nervous system, your subconscious will "kick in" to protect you. The ironic thing is that we unconsciously train ourselves to fear certain things by making false associations about their meanings. Nothing in life has any meaning but the meaning you give it. You literally create neurological links to experiences that get "stored" in your nervous system so that you can act quickly and accordingly the next time. Whenever something happens to you, you assign a meaning to it by the way you communicate the experience to yourself. Unconsciously, you are always trying to establish meaning, and at a very basic level, you are trying to establish whether something means pain or pleasure. The challenge is that when associations are reinforced, you build up beliefs that will greatly influence your behaviour and are often the cause of procrastination.

Although procrastination makes no sense intellectually, it actually reveals a lot about your unconscious and self-imposed limitations and (in)abilities. The major cause for procrastination is fear, and more specifically, the fear that taking action will lead to pain or a painful experience of some kind. At some level, your unconscious mind combines and searches its "files" to come up with a "link" that associates the action to a painful experience. This can range from something that is mildly uncomfortable to something physically painful. Although you may consciously want to do something, your unconscious will prevent you from doing it as soon as it associates pain with the action. As human beings, we automatically reach for comfort and will almost always automatically reach for whatever feels comfortable in the moment. This is why you often procrastinate on tasks that do not feel good in the moment, even though it will mean a much more pleasurable future.

Learning to push against this need for comfort is what creates all the growth that is necessary for you to really produce results. When you start to see procrastination as a blessing in disguise, you can start to use it and embrace the behavioural insights it holds for you. Procrastination reveals your fears and gives you the necessary resistance needed to expand and grow in your capacity to push past your fears and create the things you really want for your life. The quality of your life is in direct proportion to the amount of "discomfort" you can comfortably deal with. Procrastination can also shed some light on the goals that you value most, as your concern over procrastinating on it shows that some part of you care enough to be concerned.

It's been said that first, we form our habits, and then our habits form us. This is also true for habits of mind, and procrastination often manifests itself as a habitual pattern of thinking. Your thoughts lead to and help create your actions. Like the engraved pattern on a record, your behaviour will "play the same tune" every time. Your associations to pain and pleasure play an important part in your habitual behaviour in that it determines what you will or will not do. By repetition, you form habitual patterns of thinking that will cause you to automatically act or react in certain ways when your habit pattern gets triggered.

"Failure only happens when you lose your willpower to continue trying...If we let the obstacles get the best of us then it was our choice to fail, not fate."

— Lindsey Rietzsch

Being aware of your associations to pain and pleasure is critical in dealing with the root cause of procrastination. There are many symptomatic solutions that will not create a lasting result. Although you must use your willpower initially, your aim is to re-establish your associations to the tasks you are avoiding. You can be, do, or have whatsoever your heart desires, provided that you can overcome your self-imposed fears and take action. Although the real cause for procrastination resides in your unconscious mind, you are ultimately in control of your conscious actions.

The Hidden Cost of Procrastination

Be honest — are you one of those people who puts things off? It's okay, we all do it. It's human nature. "Why do something today when you can do it tomorrow," or so the saying goes. But procrastination can cost us more than we can imagine.

Why do we procrastinate? In general, we procrastinate because the task we are putting off is unpleasant in some way. Either we don't like doing it (like calling a bank), or there is some physical discomfort (like going to the dentist). The task may even be boring and monotonous, or just plain difficult.

But the effects of procrastination can run deeper than just not doing the task. Other problems it may cause are:

Being branded as lazy: When people notice that you haven't completed particular tasks, you can be branded as a lazy person. Not only can this affect your job or personal life (promotions and the like), but it may mean the tasks you really want to do are offered to someone else who is considered more reliable!

Creating clutter: Many unfinished tasks can leave a lot of clutter around—books, papers, or other items needed to perform the job.

Metal Block: So many people end up having so many thoughts and ideas running around in their mind they eventually get to a point where nothing seems to come to mind, or more importantly they can make sense of anything they want to do.

Long To-Do Lists: When a procrastinator thinks to write things down but never gets around to acting on them, the list of things they want to do gets bigger and bigger. This can often lead to lists of ideas that no longer have any value or reason.

Being bad for morale: There is nothing worse than knowing you have a job you need to do and knowing at the end of the day that the job wasn't done. It can make you feel down and even preoccupy your mind while you're trying to concentrate on other things.

Having no leeway: When you put something off, jobs accumulate. This means if an urgent task suddenly comes in, you have no leeway to drop everything and work on it, for there are too many other outstanding things that need doing.

Becoming more unpleasant: The job itself may not change by putting it off, but the feeling in our mind of how unpleasant we think the job will be grows. We think about how we have to explain not doing the job to other people, and the whole situation feeds on itself and becomes an ugly cycle.

Now, to be fair, sometimes procrastinating isn't a conscious action. Particular jobs just never seem to get done, even though you never consciously decided not to do them. But at other times, you do make the decision not to do the job at the moment and just put it off.

But you can save yourself a lot of mental clutter, and perhaps even more discomfort later on, if you just adopt a "do it now" attitude. Decide that you're just going to get the job out of the way when it comes, no matter how uncomfortable it may be. By doing the job straight away, often you will realise that the discomfort you associated with the task was simply your mind feeding on itself as you were putting it off. And the sense of relief you get from finishing the task is well worth it.

So, now that you know more about procrastination, you must ask yourself the question: "What am I going to do about it?"

Hopefully, you will decide to banish procrastination from your life and reap the rewards of that decision!

PART ONE

Planning is your Friend

Cover the Basics First

When you want to start a business, there are a few basic things you need to do in order to get the foundation. You can change these as you go, but it is important to have a foundation, somewhere to start from, and a simple structure to use and to manage. Simply thinking about it will not be enough.

Without a firm foundation, there is an ever-greater chance that something, somewhere, sometime, will fail, and what you have built will come crashing down or fail even before you begin. Look at some of the biggest structures or businesses in the world and see what sort of foundations they sit upon today.

I can almost guarantee you that they did not start on what they have now, but they most certainly started on some sort of foundation. It may have been as little as a loan from their parents with the agreement to pay it back, and until paid, the parents would oversee the use of the loan, or a group of three friends signing a simple Memorandum of Understanding together. Either way, there is almost always some sort of basic setup that is the catalyst for every business.

Some of the more important basics of starting a business are but not necessarily restricted to the following:

Choosing a business structure that you want to use. Are you a person who likes power and control? If so, you want to lean towards full ownership (a type of sole trader or 100% owner). Or do you want to have some other people invested in the business also? The structure will be everything, and you need to make sure that you get this one right from day one, as it can be a big issue later on, especially when serious decisions may need to be made. A sole owner-style position is often the best approach at first so that your vision can be developed, and then when you are ready, you can decide on a more detailed structure.

Registering for your business number and taxes. These are vital as you do not want to be getting the government or Tax Man on the wrong side of you from day one. It is better to have them on your side wherever you are rather than having them look over your shoulder and sticking their nose in unnecessarily.

Choosing a business name. Without a doubt, the most exciting part of setting up a business is the image or branding by which people will recognise you. It is one of the most exciting parts of the basic set-up and can be a defining moment in any business start-up. A good name can carry its own weight into any battle with a competitor and, given the right branding and positioning, can become an everyday word people use to describe things. Just look at Google, for example.

Setting up record-keeping and accounting systems. This is one of my least favourite parts of a business, yet it is one of the most important to get right. It is vital, and I mean *vital,* to have a good record-keeping system in place. Keeping track of your income, expenses, records, customers, etc., will help you to see where improvements can be made, where costs can be saved, and who the customers are. Everything about this basic step has an important part to play in the whole scheme of your business, so **DON'T SKIMP ON IT.**

Ensuring you understand your legal obligations. Like your taxes, you need to make sure you are aware of your legal obligations and the laws that may govern what you are doing. An engineer needs to know what laws and regulations they must work within when designing a bridge, or else the builders could be put in harm's way when construction begins. Laws have been designed to help you, not hinder you. Many people find them constraining, but in reality, many have been written based on the mistakes of the past and are there to ensure that those mistakes do not happen again.

One of the biggest mistakes people generally make, and I'm guilty of it too, is wishful thinking. You want something to be true, even if it is not true, and so you ignore the real truth because of what you want to be true. This is a very difficult trap to avoid.

Elon Musk

Arranging insurance. This is a strange one for a basic start up point, but in many cases, it will save you from headaches and pain later if it is in place. There are many different types of insurances you can get, so speak with a professional about what you may need. Start with the basics first and build upward from there. It is always important to understand that protection in all its glory can only be helpful to you so take it seriously.

Recognise Your Strengths and Weaknesses

How strong are you? How strong do you think you are? And what are your weaknesses?

This is a fundamental set of questions that most people very seldom answer honestly. We often try to over-emphasize our strengths and underplay our weaknesses because we do not want people to see the real us. We want people to see us as how we "want to see ourselves" and not what the reality is.

I am a procrastinator, through and through. To be honest, I could be a lot better off if I did not procrastinate so much. I also get sidetracked in my own projects very easily. In my work life, I am the complete opposite. I am focused and structured and work hard for my clients and the people I work for and with.

Accept yourself, your strengths, your weaknesses, your truths, and know what tools you have to fulfill your purpose."

Steve Maraboli,

Understanding your strengths and weaknesses can help you understand what you need to do and, often, what decisions need to be made. A clear understanding of these can help you focus your efforts and avoid pitfalls in the decision-making process.

Your strengths are not often what you think they are. They can be a weakness in some situations, so understanding and being aware of why they affect you can seriously be an advantage.

For some, having great structured meeting management is vital and is key to effective control. In most situations, this is needed and helps people to focus on the objectives and actionable items of the meeting. But there is always that one meeting where you want people to open up and think, to let loose and allow their imaginations to flow out all over the table. Maybe it's a research and design meeting and you are after ideas and suggestions. Being too rigid in how meetings are run in this scenario would be a killer to creative explosions.

Understanding how to use your strengths will allow you to have the best of both worlds and achieve better results. Using your strengths in the right environments at the right times can reduce your chances of messing things up.

Weaknesses also can become strengths if you know and understand them. They are the one area of almost everyone's inner sanctum that many do not want others to see and will do everything to hide them, even attempting things they are not good at to hopefully save face, only to find out that the complete devastation that follows could have been avoided had they just stepped up and owned their weakness.

There are some who say a weakness is a limitation and you should work to overcome it. I say, DO NOT DO IT. Keep the weaknesses for now. You are not wanting to start a weakness recovery program; you are wanting to start a business. Remember what I said at the start: FOCUS FOCUS FOCUS. Stay on the path to your goals. Your weaknesses will not get in the way if you know what they are and plan for them to be covered.

Once, I had to help a friend who wanted to diversify into a few new areas of his business. His business was already operating and had been successful. The one area he had problems with (his weakness) was getting his ideas onto paper. Oh, he had great ideas, and they were some of the most exciting concepts for business diversification and development I had come across, but, boy, was it hard to get them out of his head. He talked to me all the time

25

about what he wanted to do and what his plans were. We talked for weeks about these ideas. It was not until I said to him, "Nick, enough. Let's get these ideas out onto paper." That's when he said to me that this was where he had trouble.

We sat down one Wednesday afternoon, and I asked him to describe the concepts he wanted to make reality while I wrote down what he said. He told me about what he was planning to do and what he had already done to move the ideas along. To my complete surprise, he had done a massive amount of work already. He had put in place action items, met with people he would need to make his ideas a reality, and even designed new technology. Nick is an engineer and an imaginative mind ready to explode. This made me even more excited.

Once we were able to get the ideas out of his noggin, we could see the areas that needed attention. Nick was even able to modify the concepts I had written to better align with what he had been thinking. Together, we were able to create a small start towards an extremely exciting future for his business growth.

His weakness was writing, while one of my strengths is writing, so the fit was perfect.

When you finally wade through all the self-doubt and modesty, you will begin to see the following rewards of understanding your strengths and weaknesses:

- Focusing on the right things that have the most impact on your life so that your life becomes simpler.
- Your attention will focus on those areas of the project, product, or service that will create the best returns.
- You will make better decisions each and every day.
- You will be resourceful and look for opportunities to help you move ahead.
- Your results will improve as your standards increase.
- You will spend more time on areas in your life that are self-assuring and confidence-building.
- You will happily let others take some of the burden from you.
- Your stress levels will drop, and you will not feel so overwhelmed or frustrated.
- You can focus on the things you know you can do well.

"In today's society we have so many distractions and are often overwhelmed to the point where we sometimes just stop producing."

– Brian Oliver

Developing our talents is a great way to understand what we are good at and what we should leave to the experts. This practice of developing our talents is taught to us when we are young, and for some, certain things come naturally. For others, it is difficult to learn new things, particularly when they are thrust upon us by good-hearted parents who want us to succeed in life.

As we grow, learn and explore these talents, they manifest themselves in different ways. Some of the things we learnt as a child fade into the background, and some continue with us through our lives. This is where we must understand who we are and what we can do. Our strengths and weaknesses are developed based on this process of growth from childhood to adulthood.

A good way to know if you're good at something, or as my teacher used to say, "have a disposition for something", is to try it.

I tried to play the guitar and realised I could not play it well. I wanted to learn, but there was nothing in me telling me to keep it up. I bought a good guitar, thinking that if I had the right equipment, I could make it work. I even purchased a tape recording on how to play. After weeks and weeks of consideration and observation of the guitar on the stand, I realised one thing: I had to move the cassette tape so I could wipe my dresser down, or I was in trouble. The procrastinator in me held me back, and I truly believed that I could have been good, no, great. Maybe even a superstar. Nowadays, I flick a guitar string and think, man, I wasted money a lot.

On the flip side, however, I hated writing. I wasn't really good at it growing up, and so my mum would make me write out a page a night from a book. I wrote out about 10 or so books over time. They weren't super long, but man, I hated doing it. But here's the thing. As I was doing this at home every night, a change began to happen in me. I found myself being able to write at school a lot better. Not just in the use of a pen, as I had very poor handwriting, but as in comprehension, use of sentences, creativity, and imagination.

When I reached high school, I began to write my very first book (unpublished). I would write whenever I could. I even managed to get hold of a typewriter and use it to knock out a bunch of pages at a time. I was so obsessed that when I got a job as a night cashier at a petrol station, I would do all the chores as quickly as I could then I would sit and write page after page of my story.

To this day, I still find myself jotting things down for no real reason other than interest. I can't help myself, yet many of these notes have gone on to become lessons I have taught at university or in workshops. My strength in writing was not genetic, nor was it gifted to me but was taught to me by my mother. I hated writing those pages from those books, and I despised every moment I had to do it, but I thank her for what she taught me and what my mind gained from the experience.

As a business owner or a person who wants to create a product, you have to be willing to look inside and find the strengths you have. Trust me when I tell you that they are there, even if you don't think they are.

Lastly, take a moment to consider a few things about your strengths and weaknesses:

- Now that you understand your strengths and weaknesses, can you identify what you're good at? Can it work in your favour for this business idea?
- Will the business, product, or service you want to create allow you to navigate around your weaknesses in safety?
- What are the chances that additional strengths may stem and grow from certain weaknesses you have now?

It will only be when you resign yourself to accept your weaknesses and use your strengths that you will begin to see what real potential you have. Using your strengths will allow you to make right decisions and grow as a person. Accepting your weaknesses will provide you with the knowledge to seek for help when needed and accept that you simply cannot be great at everything.

Find Your Buyer First

Out there in the void, someone is waiting for you to find them. They do not know it yet, but you have just what they need. In fact, you have the very thing that may change the way they see life. A new whats-ama-do or thing-ama-bob that will make their life have even more meaning and a reason to get out of bed, or maybe it might be as simple as helping them keep their cupboard neater.

A buyer is an elusive creature. They are hidden in plain sight most of the time but go unnoticed because we do not know how to entice them out of the shadows.

Think about the business owners you know who have set up an amazing business, a great website, and flyers yet still complain about no one buying from them. Why? Because they don't know how to use these tools to find their customers, their buyers. While sales and marketing are a different topic, we will come back to it later.

What I am talking about is the "who" your product or service is aimed at. Who will be your buyers?

Understanding who these people are is a key point and the reason why it's in a section on its own.

I taught Business and Marketing at college at night for a few years while I ran a state-wide sales team for a publishing company and had an incredible time sharing my experiences.

I remember once during a class I was teaching of about 340 undergraduates, I was trying to help them understand the importance of identifying their buyers. I asked the simple question: "Who is your buyer?" Now, being an undergraduate, I was expecting some interesting answers, but I was not expecting a few of the ones I got, especially considering they were 17 weeks into their course, and we had been speaking about this topic for three weeks already. One student said, "Everyone. I want everyone to buy my product." While ambitious, there is literally no product I can think of that absolutely everyone will buy. Some come close, like toothbrushes and soap, but none that I know of would be on everyone's shopping list.

The concept that many young people forget and, in some cases, even older people misunderstand is that our Target market is not the same as our Niche.

Confused yet? Let me explain. A product or service is generally made for a specific group of people. This is called a **Target Market**. This group will fit your product or service far better than other people. It does not mean people outside the group won't buy it, but rather, they are the ones who are more likely to buy it. Don't get me wrong, though. Some of your target market will not buy either, so relax. Not everyone is ready for your awesome offering.

"Concerning Personal Branding: For the success of your brand you must know and understand i. your target market and ii. your niche. The two are not the same."

34

Bernard Kelvin Clive

You designed your product or service for someone. Who are they? Are they a 21-year-old millennial who prefers not to speak directly to people or a middle-aged white-collar worker who needs a stand-up desk? *This* is your buyer. This is the person you were thinking about when your creative thoughts came up with the product or service.

A **niche,** on the other hand, is a subset of people within your target market group. They are the ones who your product or service will really appeal to and will more than likely be the uptake in the first instance. What's more, a niche can often be made of people who fall across several target market categories or groups. Finding them and homing in on them is a bit of a skill, and there are companies out there that specialise in how to focus on these niches within your Target Market.

Diversify Your Efforts

You can never have too much diversification of your efforts. Looking for anything that can help you achieve your end goal should be something you learn to do. If you focus on one aspect of growth and development and never deviate from that, you may miss an opportunity that could help you move closer to your objective or even speed up the opportunity to reach your goal sooner.

"Not knowing when the dawn will come

I open every door."

Emily Dickinson

A good idea is to always be looking for opportunities that can help you. A few extra bucks here or a cheaper alternative for something there may just be what you need. Getting your hands dirty in the areas of your business you know nothing about is a great way to learn and be baptized by fire, so to speak.

Not everyone is apt at diversifying their efforts and some feel more comfortable on staying focused. I like to spread around and see what is out there that can help me.

When you get other people involved in **marketing** or **branding** support, do not leave it up to them just because you may not have any experience in those areas. Get involved and learn. It's your business, and you should know what's going on. Become knowledgeable in all aspects of the setup and execution. Diversify your experience and learn as you go. You will be amazed at what you pick up and what they may have missed.

Manage diversity of income with your main goal as the focus.

It is important to understand that most of your income will come from your daily job when you are starting out so whatever you do, DO NOT STOP WORKING.

Don't do what one of my clients did and think about starting a business, get some advice and then quit your job. This is mad. This is a sure way to fail from the start. Sure, you may not like your job, but it is income, and you *must* keep hold of it. It becomes the source of funds that you will need to do certain things, like living and paying rent.

You must think about how you are going to make money in the short term, especially if you want to start a business. It is often the start that has the most problems and concerns when it comes to money because this is where most of the bigger expenses are accumulated.

When I first started out on my own to create a college, I thought about it for a few months because one of the biggest issues I had was income. I felt that my time was worth something and while I was able to make a living doing what I was doing, I wanted something that would make an income for me based on work I had already done. A passive income.

I felt that I had to create a relationship with another college and utilize their license and course materials in order to allow me the time to create my own. So, I set out to find a company I could partner with. It wasn't difficult if you knew where to look, just like today. Doing some research and understanding the market you are entering is vital if you are to succeed. Once I found a company, I negotiated the deal that would benefit me from the outset. They were happy because they would make an additional 30% of income on all courses I sold and managed, irrespective of the total number of courses I sold. 1 course = 30% margin, 100 courses = 30%. Simple.

For me, though, it was a breakthrough. I had arranged to offer their courses as an onsite, workplace-centred program where students did not have to come to a classroom. They could still be working and earning their diplomas. My goal was to make the courses as student-friendly as possible while keeping them within the guidelines of the government's requirements. I managed to develop onsite programs in Business and Community

Service over a twelve-month period using the standard resources the partner college had. I started to market to businesses and community organisations and networks I knew, and within two months, I had about 50 students. Now, this may not seem like a lot, but I was earning about $75 per student per month. After expenses, that gave me an additional income of $3,750. My expenses were that I paid a tutor to train the students, and I managed the documentation and compliance work forms out of my spare bedroom.

Not bad for a two-month project to get started, and I didn't have to quit my day job either. I kept it going for another 8 months before I devoted 100% of my time to the college.

My regular income initially paid for the cost of setting up the business, a website, and marketing, as well as the costs of paper, printing, travel, and general resources (I bought a new computer, too; my wife was happy). Without that extra income, I would have struggled in the first few months.

I used some of the income I was generating to develop further networks by paying for "qualified" **lead generation,** (paying someone to find prospective clients for you) which in turn increased the signup rate by 38% over a six-month program. Was it worth it? Heck yes. That six months, signups rose to over 147 students, and I didn't even have to do so much as lift a finger.

I tried a few other small projects along the way, like a community support program for at-risk youth, which cost some money, but ultimately worked out well. It led me into a new network of community workers, all needing to upskill their credentials.

Every time I looked for or started a side project, I would always look at how it might fit into my overall goal.

"That is one of the tricks of opportunity. It has a sly habit of slipping in by the back door, and often it comes disguised in the form of misfortune, or temporary defeat."

Napoleon Hill

I asked myself some very straight-to-the-point questions, such as:

- Will this project, business, or opportunity earn me more than I am investing, including time?
- Will I be able to scale this up to where it generates more than I am currently earning in my regular job?

- How well does this fit into my overall goal and plan?
- Will this make me happy to do?

The last question is one of the most important to me. If I'm not happy doing something, then why the heck am I doing it?

I like to try things out, give things a go, and see if they work, but I also understand the importance of doing things that make you happy rather than things that just make you money. Money cannot be the only reason you do something in business.

I have to enjoy what I do. For many years I worked because I had to earn a living. I had a young family who needed my income. I had bills to pay that didn't go away no matter how often I got ahead of them. I eventually realised that if I wasn't happy with what I was doing, then I would bring that stress and frustration home, and it did not make for a happy daddy.

I eventually decided after many years of the same routine that I had to work on things that made me happy. I started college, and I loved it. I loved teaching adults, and I loved working with people to improve themselves. I am, however, not afraid as a procrastinator to admit that I don't listen to my own advice. About four years later, some decisions I made at the start of my college came back to bite me so hard that I decided to close the business, move south, and start life again.

Check the Plane Before You Take Off

There will be many things in your life that cause you concern and worry; some you can control, and some you cannot. Therefore, it is important to make sure that everything you do works or, at the very least, is in a phase that will allow it to work when implemented.

Look at an airplane: how often does it get serviced? How often does the fuel system get checked? Are the brakes working? Do the flaps move correctly according to the input controls used by the pilot? One might consider that an airplane is bound to have issues on a regular basis simply because of its size and complexity. How safe is it, really?

The question has often come into my mind when I have had to take a plane somewhere, and I sit in my seat and feel myself gripping the handles just a little bit tighter as the cabin begins to rumble and the sound of the engine roars to life, lifting the massive body and all aboard into the lofty skies above. I'm taking a one-hour trip to somewhere like Sydney for work, yet on some flights, I feel like I have had to put my life on the line to do so.

This is exactly how I feel about business, or, more precisely, new business ideas and **ventures**. I know the work is right. I know that the plans and procedures are in place to make sure that everything goes smoothly. Yet when the time comes, I still feel that slight rise in adrenalin and anxiety like I do when I fly.

The difference is that you are responsible for making sure that you have checked and double-checked all the elements that go into launching your business. If it's your business, don't leave it in the hands of someone else. Get out and get dirty. Make sure that things are in the right order, that suppliers are in place, manufacturing is ready and operational, and most of all that your plan is following the course you have set.

If any one of the elements of a business is faulty and in need of attention, it could mean the difference between a successful take-off or a spectacular crash that might see everything around you go up in flames.

Not to be a buzzkill, but just like a 747, your business has to have a strong maintenance plan and team that can service the areas that need attention, especially when starting out. This is where most of the problems will arise, and it is your job, along with the people you hire, to make sure things run smoothly.

Now, this may be a bit contradictory to other parts of this book, but don't be in too much of a rush to get going. Factor in the things that make the business run and work effectively to ensure they are operations and effective as best as they can possibly be.

Here are some ideas to help with the maintenance and preparation of your business. These are very similar to what you may do should you own a 747 but I think they work just as well for businesses.

There are two main critical functional models of maintenance: preventive maintenance and requirement-based maintenance. In Preventive Maintenance, extra steps are usually taken to protect the business from snags that could possibly occur in the future, like procedural inspection to foresee and rectify processes that could possibly create problems in the future.

Requirement-Based Maintenance involves rectifying the problem as and when it occurs, i.e., it is requirement-specific. It usually involves critical activities, so instructions are usually prepared proactively for many foreseen problems to ensure minimum time wastage during its occurrence.

Process and Procedure Testing is a critical operational activity that management and staff should perform. Every part, such as the website, marketing posters, brochures, and store appearance, is inspected and immediately replaced or improved if found problematic.

Testing procedures are usually repetitive, complex and meticulously designed. These procedures are divided into certain levels depending upon the kind of maintenance your business needs. Under normal conditions, a business should be inspected or have an internal Audit every 6 months in my opinion, even more often in some cases. Many experts suggest getting a thorough Audit done every 12 months, but it really depends.

Taking Client satisfaction into account, Business Maintenance has never been considered an ordinary daily activity. This is because many businesses seem to run smoothly and show no signs of problems until it's too late. Doing a few checks and balances on your processes and procedures can often help resolve an issue that may not seem problematic but may turn into one if nothing is done about it.

One quick addition to this point I want to make, considering that we live in a digital world is the importance of maintenance of your website. It is an absolute necessity to keep it fresh for visitors. Maintaining your website means updating it with fresh content, great images, and stories, keeping it free from errors, and maintaining a high position in search engines. Your goal is to keep them on your site for as long as you can. This is where updated and interesting content is king.

Once your site is live, you may need some to keep it updated. Sometimes it is a simple change, like changing a date, or adding a new section or some other modifications. It may seem tiresome to do, but rest assured, updated content is always more interesting to a customer than old, worn-out stories. It is much like going into a waiting room and seeing piles of old, worn-out magazines sitting there. Torn, battered, and in need of recycling. It's not inviting to the customer. Yes, they may flick through, but that's because they have nothing else to do. Sadly, for a Digital presence, it's as simple as going to another website.

Web maintenance services by a third party can substantially reduce your costs by eliminating the need to hire full-time web design professionals or programmers.

Their services often include-

1. Keeping your site up-to-date: search engines will more regularly spider your site, if the content is continuously updated. Adding a new article in every week may solve the problem. Other updating involves changing information regarding products, services, prices-which will keep your visitors informed.

2. Checking for broken links: Broken links upset visitors, making them click elsewhere. You will lose potential customers if they are not checked properly.

3. Managing your site: With the help of new technologies, a vendor can make changes that will improve your site's performance. New innovative features must be added from to time.

4. Re-structuring your site: Using your site access statistics like the number of visitors visited daily and what they really want from your site, a vendor/third party can

help you re-structure your site contents for increased business.

5. Writing correct and clean HTML code: HTML errors can negatively affect your search engine rankings.

Depending on the frequency, you need to update your site; you can make a contract with a vendor. For small business owners, who occasionally need a vendor, pay-as-you-go is a perfect way to work this into your budgets. You can pay them hourly, weekly, monthly or yearly-as per your workload.

There are plenty of companies out there offering this service, so get online and have a look.

Hand Ups, Not Hand Outs

I thought about this section long and hard because I considered it to be a typical analogy that everyone uses. Yet when I sat and thought about it, I realized that it is one of the most profound points about development and growth you can learn.

We all know the analogy that you can give someone a fish and feed them for a day, or you can teach a person to fish and feed them for life. But this simple statement is one of mixed confusion for some.

Teaching someone to fish does not give them food for life but rather merely gives them the skill to obtain food. It allows them the basic understanding of what is required but does nothing to help them understand the aspects of finding the fish or anything else once they have a fish.

I know this may seem a bit pessimistic, but let me explain. In the business world of a procrastinator, knowledge is not often the problem. We know what we want, we have studied the processes, the skills, and the understanding of what we want, but we lack one fundamental point: the understanding of how or even where to start. Sure, we could figure this out too, but I believe this is where a procrastinator comes unstuck.

When you know what you want but you don't know where to start or even have the real motivation to actually get started, then a simple distraction is all that is required to get you off track, and this pattern continues to happen time and time again.

My solution to this is to GET HELP. Find someone you can work with to set a plan in place. Planning is easy at the start and only gets harder as you go.

"Plan for what is difficult while it is easy, do what is great while it is small. The difficult things in this world must be done while they are easy, the greatest things in the world must be done while they are still small."

Sun Tzu

Give yourself some goals and ask the questions early about some of the challenges you may face. Put your hand up and ask the questions you need answers to, and if you cannot find someone to answer them, then go to the internet. I have heard it said that "Dr Google knows everything." Well, that may be right to some extent, so why not use its knowledge?

Five points about hand ups for business are these:

- Learn what you can use from the resources around you
- Do some research on what additional things you need for your business
- Work these resources and information into your plans

- Develop the strategies to achieve your goal(s)
- Set a date for when you will start

Once you have done that, study the information and then study it again until it is embedded in your mind so tightly that you live it and breathe it.

When it comes down to the crux of it, don't let people just give you information and resources without understanding how they can benefit your business and how they can work inside your plans. If you do, you might end up with two things: a rod but no idea where to use it or some fish you have no idea how to cook.

Do not be afraid to ask for help. When you need advice, go to the people who know the information you're after and ask. Many people in business go straight to the CEO or General Manager, bypassing their own bosses. It's funny too, because some of those people may never have met the top brass of the business, but they are not afraid of being embarrassed: in fact, they are confident and willing to step out of their comfort zone to get an answer. But bear in mind that you need tact when doing this. Be mindful of their time and workload, and where possible, arrange a meeting rather than walking in on them. It is important to remember that making a nuisance of yourself is no way to win friends and influence people.

As a prospective business owner, you must be willing to *step out in order to step up*. Many people have come before you and many people will come after you, so don't be so arrogant to think that you are the prime candidate for being smart and going to the top first. You're not.

Naturally, if you're ambitious and your ideas are sound, then you are going to want to go to the top for the right answers. I have reached out to many people at the top of their fields and asked them for counsel or information. Most answer vaguely and some never at all, but those that do are so informative it's like getting gold from a mine shaft. Precious nuggets of pure bliss right there on the paper. Or email.

I have a running joke with my wife about a little thing called the Oprah Rule. My wife will often ask me for advice, or she will talk to me about something she heard or read, and I will weigh in on what I know about the topic, sharing my thoughts and imparting my precious nuggets of truth to her. She will often disagree with me about certain things and think, or should I say, tell me that my thoughts are wrong or inaccurate. I have learnt to let that water run right off this duck's back. A few days or sometimes weeks later, she'd be watching Oprah Winfrey, and the exact topic my wife was speaking to me about would be on the show. Oprah would give the same advice, guidance, or answers that I gave, and my wife would lap it up like it's the elixir of eternal life. She will catch me watching her, and we will both laugh. See, to my beautiful wife, Oprah is all-knowing on these matters, whereas I am just some guy who pays the bills.

When you are asking people for help, there are a few things you should remember. Here are some helps I have come across over the years that I should have listened to more clearly as well:

Be clear about what you are asking. If you are going into a business to talk to them about selling your products, then tell them that. Don't beat around the bush. People have neither the time nor the patience to listen to waffle. Use statements like, "I want to be able to send people to you to buy my products" instead of "I want you to sell my products so I make money." I am sure you will get a more positive reception.

Don't try to schedule a meeting the next day if you just met someone. Most businesspeople have calendars and their weeks laid out in advance. They are caught off guard when someone asks them to set up an appointment the following day or even a few days later. Give them time to plan and fit you in. More often than not, I tell people that I will send them an email to discuss when a suitable time will be rather than trying to get them to commit on the spot.

Do some homework on the company or person you are wanting to see. It is unprofessional when you don't know who you are talking to. However, if you are going straight for the top and reaching out to the powers that be in a big organization, you need to know who they are going in. If you want to place your products with a company, then the CEO is not the person you should speak with, but rather the procurement manager or operations manager in many cases.

Always be willing to give something in return. This is where you have to think about what you can offer the company that makes them want to do business with you. Offer them marketing space on your website, or free publicity at an event or expo space. Giving enticements can often help cement a good deal.

Do not overshoot or oversell the target. Be incredibly careful that you are not going too big for the sake of going big. Sure, it is fun and can be an adventure, but remember that you may only get one chance at it, so you must make a good first impression. Once you have secured the deal, stop talking. Over-selling is just bad practice.

Be the person people want to help. Make it easy for people to want to work with you. Give them reasons to be your solution. Whatever you offer, be willing to be the contact person for it so they don't have to worry about customer follow-up or concerns. Offer support and information on the products to continue to keep them informed and up to date.

Don't ask for a job. Do not walk in sounding needy and desperate to make the deal work. People see it and feel it in your pitch. Be confident but not over the top. There can often be a perception that you need them more than they need you. You want the latter. They need to think they need your product or service. This way, you are in the driving seat.

Be confident and professional – even when falling off the cliff. Many company CEOs, managers, and buyers will often say no at the outset to see how you handle disappointment. They are looking for your reaction to see your response. Show gratitude for the meeting even if it does not go your way. Let them know you are ready when they are, and stay positive. They may just call you back when they see your product or service taking off in the market.

Rivals are Great. They Build Your Revenue

I have watched so many people falter because of competitors and get scared off because they think the threat of a rival is too great. This is so far from what you should do it's crazy to consider.

Oh wait, that's right! This may be a reason why we procrastinate.

When we stop looking at rivals as our competitors, we can see the opportunities they may have missed, and even see the flaws in what they may have done. It opens your eyes to a world free from the care of what others are doing and allows you to explore the possibilities of your own goals and objectives.

I never consider a rival company as a competitor. I look at them as someone I can learn from, someone I can gain valuable knowledge from and sidestep mistakes I may have made had they not existed. I stop focusing on what they do better than me and what they have achieved and instead focus on how I can do what they are doing…but better.

Dharmesh Shah, co-founder and CTO of HubSpot, writes, "You are often your biggest competitor. You should not completely ignore your competition, but the biggest battle happens inside the four walls of your start-up's office. Start-ups come down to pure execution of a strategy on a daily basis and maintaining the faith for the long haul. Most start-ups don't lose to competition, but because they lose the will to fight."

Too many people focus on things they cannot control, like a rival with a brand-new gizmo or gadget or money, which in turn creates potential self-doubt.

With the old me, it would be a case of a sudden lack of motivation to keep going. I used to think, what's the point? I don't have the money to compete against them or that. I would spend so much time looking at how others were doing it and how successful they were that I slowly lost focus and eventually would move on to something else. It was a serious issue I had, and I could not seem to get past it.

Then when the light finally came on, I began to realise that I was my own worst enemy. I had let my own self-doubt and my own irrational beliefs stop me from doing what I had wanted to do. I had literally let my competitors' actions dictate my own, and what was worse was that they didn't even know they were destroying a competitor. I was their tool in destroying myself.

Once you can get past the emotions of worrying about your competitors, you begin to see what you can achieve. You begin to understand that a competitor is a valuable tool full of research and knowledge that you simply have to watch in order to learn.

Look at what they do to gain customers. What they do to increase their branding? What do they do to grow their social presence? They have made the mistakes, they have failed, and they have gotten back up with fresh understanding. This is free knowledge you can use. Your competitors are a total gold mine of resources if you look at them that way.

In fact, if you're smart, you will even work out from your rivals what they can do for you to make you more money. That's right. Your competitors can make you money if you use them correctly. But that's another story.

Many successful entrepreneurs work well under pressure. They have this uncanny ability to view pressure not as an obstacle but more as an opportunity. Competition is good even if, over time, your competitors are trying to undercut you or push you out of the market. When this happens, it's a great time to take advantage of a few key points:

- User your team's talents and learn from them. They will often have insights into your competitors that you do not see. Take time to learn from them and use what they know in productive ways to boost your own business.
- Build a business that would be hard to compete against. Have clout in the industry and stand out from your competitors. Let them keep you on your toes.
- Remain positive about what you are trying to achieve and look for ways to grow through developing strong and meaningful partnerships. Alliances in business can often

shield you from your competitors' advances and attacks. Through the exchange of technology and tools, you can work to develop products and services faster. In fact, this often leads to an even stronger product launch and allows you to speed up your timeline to success.

Look at your industry's current climate and seek out industry trends or niches. There will always be someone out there working on something better than you, so you need to be on top of it when it appears. Don't try to take on an entire industry; rather, focus on a specific element or area that shows promise and growth potential.

Without competitors, most businesses get lost in the day-to-day grind we all like to call the office. As new and innovative companies join the market, you will need to start challenging yourself to accomplish more, to reach out and be explorers, to try new things, and to use your imagination to stay ahead.

Instead of focusing your energy on outdoing the competition, make sure that you invest in becoming a truly customer-centred business. This way, you will boost customer loyalty and can easily defend against aggressive suppliers or vendors who are only focused on stealing your hard-earnt clients. At the end of the day, it is your customers – not your competitor – that have the power to make or break your business, so treat them like they are everything to you. A good business owner will have great service and respect for those who pay his wages.

Avoid letting rivalries turn sour and negatively impact your business. Invest in taking full advantage of the opportunities available when there are other companies targeting the same audience and buyer.

Competition in the business world is often viewed as a negative thing, but it doesn't have to be. Remember, competition can benefit you and especially your customer!

Let's look at some of the ways in which competitors can help you if you are willing to use them to your advantage:

They prevent you from becoming lazy and overly comfortable in your business practices. It's easy to feel confident and relaxed in your business if you have a unique product that everyone wants. You don't feel any pressure to better yourself or your product. Everyone wants it, so it must be good as it is, right? Then, one day, another company comes along that begins offering similar products that are just a little bit better than yours. Uh-oh!

Now you feel the pressure to perform. You don't want to lose your customers, so you need to continuously improve your product and your level of customer service. You now need to give your customers a stronger reason to keep coming back to you.

They encourage you to be more creative. So, now you're not the only one selling purple-polka-dotted purses anymore. What can you do? Develop more products! Stretch your imagination. Come up with some unique ideas that will either improve upon your existing products or design new ones. Come up with a line of new accessories, new colour schemes, new sizes, and styles. Don't try to copy what your competitors are doing; do something different and unique. Express your own creativity.

They help you to stretch out of your comfort zones. Perhaps you have a solid customer base and haven't had to invest much in promoting your company until now. But the attention is slowly beginning to drift away from you. Now, you need to work a little harder at your level of visibility. You can advertise some sales or special promotions, get more involved with your local community, or donate a portion of sales to a worthy cause. Become as visible as you can in your community. Whether you have an online business or a brick-and-mortar one, you need to remain in your customers' minds. Put yourself and your company out there whenever you can. Be noticeable, be memorable.

They force you to charge reasonable prices. This may sound like a bad thing, but it's not. Think of yourself as a **consumer**. Aren't you always looking for good value for your money? Of course you are. And so are your customers! While it's great to be earning a lot of money for your products, you also want to be fair to your customers if you want them to come back again. No one likes to feel like they're being over-charged or ripped off. You may need to explore different suppliers and materials in order to keep your prices in line, but your customers will thank you for it by returning again and again.

Joint ventures. These can be extremely profitable for both parties if they're done right. Perhaps you and your competitor can offer discounts to the other's customers and do some cross-promotion for each other. Promote your competitor's purses, and she will promote your scarves and shoes. Swap ads in each other's newsletters. Think of some ways in which both of you could work together to benefit yourselves, as well as your customers.

Build each other up, rather than trying to tear each other down.

These concepts become a little more challenging when applied to distributors who work for the same company, but it's still possible to find ways to work together in growing your businesses. Perhaps you can co-host a home-business seminar and share in the product sales and recruits. Share the costs of advertising in a prominent publication and split the responses. Or each of you can target different markets and give referrals to each other. Working together will ultimately result in more sales for your company, which will benefit both of you also!

Competition can seem threatening at times, but the truth is, there is room for all of us! Just think about the popular burger places in the world today. I can think of at least 4 or 5 well-known ones, including the two most popular that are usually found within blocks of each other in any city -- or sometimes right next door to each other! These companies earn billions of dollars a year. Look at how these companies keep encouraging each other to do better. In their competition, they are creating menus that have items for only $1, new value meal combinations, new sandwiches and salads, later hours, and more. It's benefitting the consumer by giving them more choices and better value for their money, and it's benefitting the burger places by earning them more money. It's a win-win situation all around.

So the next time you see one of your competitors, smile, wave, and say, "THANKS!"

"When dealing with people, let us remember we are not dealing with creatures of logic. We are dealing with creatures of emotion, creatures bristling with prejudices and motivated by pride and vanity."

Dale Carnegie

POSSIBLE is an Eight-Letter Word

Ask yourself one question: what's it going to take? This question was something I needed to ask long ago from never starting a business. I would sit in front of my computer or at the table and sketch out dozens of calculations on what it would cost to do this, or how many of these I needed to get there.

Writing down all of these things is great if you want to have a book full of ideas, but they literally get you nowhere if you do not act upon them.

Eventually I went back and looked at those ideas and flicked through the pages of weird little notes or outlandish ideas I had and resolved myself to the room in my head entitled "Too Hard."

In relation to business, I used to think that there were things that were impossible to do. Things that little ol' me would never or could never achieve. I mean, I really didn't have the capacity to take on industry giants, so why bother trying to go up against them? It's impossible, right?

No, it's not. Those notes are the start of something your brain is trying to tell you. This is what I like to call the Possibility Brain Leak.

When you think something is possible, remember to follow this acronym I came up with: **POSSIBLE,** which stands for **Planning Opportunities Stand Stronger In Becoming Legitimate Enterprises.**

I was fairly young, maybe 16, when I first coined this acronym, and I remember that I had to write an assignment on what I thought about whether planning out a business in a business plan was worth the time. I don't know what I wrote in the assignment, but I do remember coming up with this term, POSSIBLE, because it stuck with me all this time.

I have had so many ideas racing around my mind over the years that if I was to draw them out, it would look like a maze encircling me. Somewhere in there, though, would be the one idea that would catapult me to the highest reaches of my dreams. Just how to find it is the struggle I have.

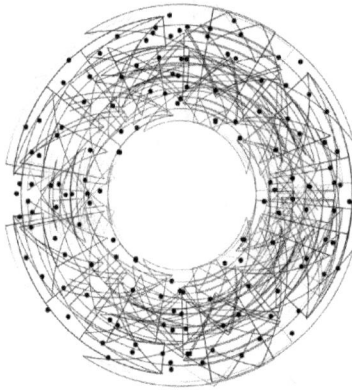

I never really shared it with people because I even felt it sounded a bit funny, but I tell you, it helped me understand concepts many times through my education.

I recall once I was teaching a university class at Griffith University, and one of my students was having a real hard time understanding the concept of planning a business and the effort needed to do this. She always seemed to be lost in lecturers and, from what I could tell, not grasping terms in business at all. She had not done too well on one of her assignments and her tutor had told me she might not pass at all. I did not like to see kids fail, so I thought I needed to bring out the big guns. It was time for me to launch the POSSIBLE acronym on the world.

She came up to me after the class where I had used my POSSIBLE acronym (I have always been proud of it) and said it had made sense. She said that she understood that planning does not mean all opportunities will work or even succeed but that by doing it, the chances of finding the right opportunity have a better chance of showing its face. Spot on, I told her.

I found out that after that class, students must have loved the acronym because, for the next few months, I would see it pop up every so often in an assignment here or there. I sort of felt proud of my creation because now it seemed to have legitimacy and not sound like a goofy term a kid made up. Anyway, weeks went by, and then one day, I was sitting at my desk, ready for class, and a young student came in. I'll call her Kasey. She said, "Mr Ferguson, I have been thinking about that story you told us about how you came up with the acronym POSSIBLE. Do you realise that you also created the IMPOSSIBLE too?"

I said, "I'm not sure what you are talking about. It's POSSIBLE, not IMPOSSIBLE". Who was this whippa snapper to get my creation wrong? I mean, seriously, (Not really, but I wanted to add some effect here). "What do you mean?" I asked. Kacey pulled out her notebook and turned to a very full page. At the top of the page was my name (feeling good). Underneath this was the title of the Class, "POSSIBLE IS AN EIGHT LETTER WORD." To the left of this was a small note, "Love this guy's class," and beside it was another note, obviously from another student, as it was a different pen, and handwriting. "Me too" (Feeling even happier).

Other than the notes about my awesome teaching abilities, the page was a complete mind explosion of notes, small diagrams, and comments. I looked at it then said, "What am I looking at?" She said look and pointed to a highlighted quote I must have made during the class.

"Information makes the planning of opportunities stand stronger in becoming legitimate enterprises (experiences)."

I looked at the page, then up at her, then at the page, then up at her. She smiled and crossed out the word "the and the word "of" in the highlighted section. "Your POSSIBLE is also IMPOSSIBLE. I figured that you mean that the impossible enhances the possible by forcing us to find more information." I thought to myself, "Holy crap. She's right. It does, I did, It can." I sat back like a refined academic and said, "Yes, that's exactly what I meant; well done." (Still trying to keep the excitement from bursting out).

So now we have: IMPOSSIBLE: **Information Makes Planning Opportunities Stand Stronger In Becoming Legitimate Enterprises.**

This is a key element in how I think these days. I mean, I know some things seem impossible right now, but that is only because we have not cracked the code to get rid of the part that limits our ability to think beyond the impossible. We have not collected enough information to allow us to plan and work towards a legitimate outcome.

I'm sure the Wright brothers did not sit around and suddenly one day think, let's make a plane. It was information and planning that preceded the great flight Orville took on December 17, 1903. Even though the flight was only 120 feet and lasted 12 seconds, the IMPOSSIBLE had suddenly become POSSIBLE.

This little book of information and planning you are reading seems so much sweeter than just words on a page to me. It is a dream that has been in the making for over 30 years. I always wanted to write a book but never figured I would get around to it. Well, the impossible in my mind is now possible.

Oh, and yes, Kacey passed her course with flying colours, all thanks to hard work and the POSSIBLE she made IMPOSSIBLE. (Did you like that?)

Diligent Homework is Vital

I cannot begin to stress this enough: make sure you exercise Due Diligence.

Many people rush into a business idea with guns blazing and jump at every little action they think will catapult them even further ahead without taking a long, hard look at the value proposition or the benefits that the action may have for them.

"The men who will act today and the men who will act tomorrow get beaten by the men who acts now."

— *Amit Kalantri*

A smart person spends time looking over the facts of the actions, assessing the angles of play from competitors and suppliers alike, watching how the market reacts to similar products or services. This is how you can learn to use information to your advantage instead of having it used against you.

I have learnt to look at several key areas that should be considered, and they are what I like to call the IPPPPS Principle (yes, another acronym of mine).

IPPPPS stands for: Intellectual Property, People, Premises, and Providers.

When it comes to your business, what you know and what you have developed are some of, if not the most valuable, assets you have. Make sure that you have your documents in place. If you need a patent on something, then get one. Do not wait till later or when you have money for it. You may lose the chance later as the market can move very quickly when something new enters the room.

A Patent is the way people and companies protect their intellectual property and ideas. Without a patent in place, people can create the same product and sell it without any infringement. Protecting your ideas is worth the money and saves you a lot of hassle if you try to chase someone who is using your idea. Sometimes trying to prove it was your idea (when there is no patent in place) can often cost more than the original patent would have cost.

And while not directly your IP, if you are working with suppliers of equipment or manufacturers, make sure they are the legal owners of the parts you use or that there is a clear and defined legal path that can be identified. You can never protect your IP enough.

When you start out, you are going to want to start cheap and save money on employing people you may know or people with not as much experience as others, simply because you think you can pay them less. But remember this: cheap is not always best.

As you move forward, it may be the front-line workers that drive the business forward through hard work and effort, and the success will be coming off of their shoulders. I suggest taking a hard look at the people you employ and asking yourself whether they meet the standards you want to set or are able to meet them. After all, it will be their knowledge that will help inspire growth of your idea and dream, and it will be their hard work and effort that will be a driving force.

When it comes to location, there are two simple rules we all need to follow:

1. Your business may be reliant on a good location.
2. That location needs to be seen as part of the family and not just where you work.

It's weird to consider a premise as a person or an entity that you can have a relationship with, but I have seen several very promising businesses fall over because of their decision to occupy a certain premise contrary to the cries of those around them.

I have firsthand knowledge of someone who took up a lease on a facility simply because of its low lease fees and close proximity to their home. While the logic was sound to keep lease fees down, the result was that after several months of occupying the facility, the council came in and said they could not operate from the location because the zoning of the areas was, in fact, agricultural and not industrial. Sadly, they had to move to a facility in the right zoning and at almost 3 times the cost. Fortunately, things worked out, and they grew well. It was a crazy experience to be in and watch, but it taught me a valuable lesson.

Do your homework and check leases before you sign them. Make sure that the location meets your needs. Don't settle on OK. Find the location that will make you want to base jump off the Sydney Harbour Bridge. Location is everything, emotionally and strategically.

Suppliers and the businesses you work closely with should also be scrutinised (in a quiet and respectful way, of course) to ensure that you are dealing with the right type of people.

I am a Chief Consultant for an investment advisory group where I evaluate the merits, practicality, and future potential of projects or opportunities presented to them. One of the main areas I focus on is the suppliers to the project or proposal. One very interesting area that is a classic example of when doing your homework is so important is when you are trying to buy chicken wings from Brazil.

I am telling you it is one of the hardest things to do because of the number of fake and misleading brokers out there.

I was asked to do some research on a deal that had been presented to my colleague on a very lucrative deal. So they gave me the names of the brokers and companies involved in the proposal to secure one hundred tons of chicken feet that would head to Hong Kong worth about US$2.2 million a month on a 12-month contract. On my request, they also gave me a copy of the Letter of Offer and several emails they had received over the last 3 weeks.

So, the first thing I did was look up all the company names on the documents, the names of all the people who had signed the document (on the seller's side) or who had been mentioned, and any other titles of businesses or locations listed. In less than two hours, I was able to put together a two-page report on my discoveries.

Using Google, Facebook, LinkedIn, Pinterest, and YouTube, I found out that the CEO of the brokerage firm was a scam artist and had been involved in several other ventures like this. I was able to identify the name of the actual company and where they were located, the name of the managing director, who had signed the proposal offer, as well as their favourite food. In fact, by the end of my research, I was able to link the people from the proposal to the actual bank account business name being used and show that none of the companies had been in business longer than a year even though on their website they claimed to be "the largest importer of food into Asia."

It means a lot to people when you can save them from a US$580,000 deposit that was most assuredly going to disappear all because of exercising some due diligence.

There is a book called *Write Your Business Plan* by The Staff of Entrepreneur Media, Inc. where they talk about the need to better understand the reasons consumers will buy your product. They go through things such as consumer behaviour and cultural, societal, and personal factors that influence that behaviour. Therefore, doing homework is so important when launching a new product, developing a unique service, or simply looking to enter into a new market.

When conducting research into a new venture, market research should be a priority, not a desire. So many companies fall short of proper research that they fail to see the plain truths before them. Their homework is only as good as their willingness to cut corners and budgets to save a few cents.

Let's talk for a moment about how effective research can save you a fortune in money and mistakes.

There are two types of **market research**: *primary* and *secondary*.

We should all know that primary research studies what customers do and buy directly, whereas secondary research is the study of information that others have gathered about customers. That's right, your competitors will have done some of the work for you, so use it. There are so many ways to do primary research. I'm not going to go into them in this book, but I will say this: without it, you're treading on very thin ice, and the risks of not knowing how thick that ice is will most certainly cause you to fall through at some point.

When you are conducting market research, there are a few questions you should consider trying to answer. You may not answer all of them directly, but you should at least try to as best you can.

The basic questions you'll try to answer with your market research include:

- Who are your customers?
- What are the items that they're buying?
- What are their buying habits relating to your product or service, including how much they may buy?
- Who is their favourite supplier?
- Why do they buy?

Now, I know some of you will focus your market research on your customers, and this is good. However, the other side to that coin is your competitors. Do not forget about them.

Finding out about your industry helps you better understand how things are currently operating, the successes that are being had and the purposes for why the industry does what it does. You need to consider aspects such as:

- Who is of a similar size to you now?
- What companies are located and operating in the same geographic location as you are?
- Do they have a similar business structure?

What is the age of your closest competitors? Remember, age occasionally has nothing to do with the result. Collecting good data on the market, your competitors, and the industry allows you to understand how much meat is left on the bone for you when you first start. You may not flood the market from day one, but if you do your homework, you can figure out which part of the bone is going to give you the most meat.

There are four key points to remember also when venturing out into the work of market research. It is going to cost some money, so spend wisely. These four points are in no specific order, but they can help you save time and money on the journey:

Prioritise what you want to achieve in the first place. Don't waste time on nonstarter ideas. Focus and make clean strategies. It's impossible to research everything so focus on the information and collection strategy that is going to give you the biggest bang for your buck.

Determine what you need to research from the start. The more you have a clear understanding of what you are trying to research, the better your results will be. The value in the research is that it can give you answers to things you may not have been looking for, so decide early what you want to know.

Do not discard less expensive approaches. Failure to consider all possible angles to research just because it does not sound expensive is a sure-fire way to waste your budget. There are entire organisations out there, like trade unions, chambers of commerce, and small business centres that will have done a hell of a lot of research already, so go and grab it.

You may be a good alternative to use for research. Do not discount the fact that you may be a very cost-effective way of gathering research. Nowadays, a few good hours in front of the internet can produce some surprising results. Don't pay for someone to do some research that you could just as easily and inexpensively do.

"Your never-ending to-do list will become a bit less intimidating once its contents are prioritized."

Adam Torren

When you're doing your research, make your homework count. Everything you do should be about getting results. All information is important and can help you, but structures and focused research will produce the best results.

Lose the Battle to Win the War

In any business start-up, you are going to have defeats, and these defeats or losses will rip you up inside if you let them. So don't let them. Instead, use them to your advantage. Make sure that the loss is your gain and that the focus of your objective never changes.

In many strategic encounters, military leaders would prefer to lose the battle in order to win the war. Sometimes, this phrase is taken out of context, and people may tell you that you *have* to lose a battle to win a war. What a load of rubbish.

Optimism is thinking you can win at all costs, and pessimism is thinking you must or will lose. Both have inherent dangers in them.

You do not have to lose a battle, but rather know when it's time to withdraw. If you go into business thinking that you must lose a battle, what your subconscious will do is continue to look for the losing battle instead of trying to win. Let your brain focus on the end goal rather than the crazy notions of mandatory defeat.

You can find yourself so caught up in not losing that you will miss the opportunities that you need to succeed. They simply pass you by because you stopped looking for them due to always trying to win.

There will come a time when you must face two decisions: one may be a short-term loss for a long-term gain and the other will be a long-term loss for a short-term gain. When the gains are money, this decision can quickly be the deciding factor for success of failure in a new business.

Deep down — and I mean deep, deep down, way past our conscious brain — we're programmed to see optimism as expensive folly and pessimism as gritty reality.

"None of my ancestors — or yours — contributed to our DNA by thinking 'yeah, there's probably no lion around the next corner'."

Scott Phillips

I have been in meetings where so-called professional development gurus tell you that to succeed when you're being chased by a bear because he wants your fish, you don't have to outrun the bear. You just have to outrun the other guy.

That advice is just useless rubbish. The best option is to not even be there in the first place. Therefore, you need to pick your battles. Keep an eye out for the 340kg mass of fur and claws coming at you. Trust me—if you are on the ball with your business, you will see it coming from a mile away. Recognizing what to do with it is when the so-called battle is won or lost.

Sally Percy, a contributor at Forbes and Workopolis, has a few very good questions to ask yourself before going into battle:

1. Is this your battle to fight?

Thinking that you have to fight a battle that actually belongs to someone else is a very easy mistake to make. Sometimes, you can get involved in another person's battle without even meaning to. Alternatively, you might be the kind of person who likes to "stick up for" your more timid colleagues. Resist falling into this trap at all costs. If it's someone else's battle, then someone else needs to be fighting it. You have enough battles of your own to contest.

2. What difference will winning this battle make in the long term?

To answer this question, you need to take a step back and look at the big picture. That might mean the strategy of your organization or what's happening in the wider world. It might mean your relationship with a superior or a line report. It might mean the direction of your career in general. When you consider the possible outcomes of this battle, how do they impinge on the bigger picture? If winning the battle might help your team to perform better, it's probably worth fighting, provided you go about it in the right way. On the other hand, you don't want to put your job on the line for something that makes little difference in the long run.

3. What happens if I lose this battle?

Before you go into battle, it's always a good idea to understand the possible downside risks. What's the worst that could happen? Could you compromise your place in the team or become unpopular with colleagues? Could you inadvertently create bad feelings over an issue that is ultimately not that important? Could you harm the prospects of the company? Are these all risks that you are prepared to take? An evaluation of the downsides is not a reason to avoid going into battle, but weighing the downsides against the upsides in a clear-headed fashion will help you to identify if it is a battle worth fighting at all.

4. Why does this matter?

Does it matter because you want to be right, or does it matter because everything is going to FALL APART – or at least go very wrong – if things don't go your way? If people are going to lose a lot of money or be hurt if you lose, that is a good reason to go to battle. If you just want to be right, that's not a good enough reason to go to war.

I mean, people do it all the time, but it's always a bad decision.

4.a. If the answer to Question 1 was "Because everything is going to FALL APART – or at least go very wrong- if things don't go my way," ask yourself this: are you sure you don't just want to be right?

5. Could I be wrong?

Think about this very hard. Are you always right? Have you ever been wrong in your life? Could this be one of those times? Listen to the other side of the argument and ask yourself if there might be some reason on that side. I'm not saying you're wrong, but it is possible. Keep in mind that fighting, winning, and then turning out to be wrong might be worse than losing.

6. What am I going to do if I don't win?

Before any negotiation, ask yourself what you will do if you don't reach an agreement at the current bargaining table. What are some realistic courses of action available? Researching and knowing these alternatives–yours and theirs–is your source of power.

7. Can I win?

Here's the thing: even if you're right, there might be no possibility – or only a very small possibility – of you winning, in which case you have to weigh the stakes and decide whether it's worth it.

8. Is it really worth the stress?

Here's where you go back to Question 1. Fighting for what you want can damage relationships and cause problems. It can also be incredibly rewarding and change things for the better. Ask yourself if the potential fallout is worth it. The answer will probably be obvious if you are honest with yourself. If lives will be destroyed if things don't go your way, it's worth fighting, even if you're very unlikely to win. If you will lose allies and the only potential fallout if your bruised ego, it's not worth it.

9. If you don't fight this battle, regardless of whether you win it or lose it, will you be able to live with yourself afterward?

This is the killer question because your conscience should play a key role in determining the battles that you choose to contest. There is nothing laudable about running away from a battle that you know, in your heart, needs to be fought. Even if it upsets your boss. Even if it makes you unpopular with your peers. Even if you are a potential whistle-blower, the battle you are preparing to fight could bring down your business. At the end of the day, you need to be able to look yourself in the mirror and believe that you made the decision that seemed genuinely right at the time. You will only achieve that by asking this very important question.

The issue I have with this is that it's not actually a battle you're losing. It's a decision not to get into the battle in the first place. That is not a loss. It is a strategic decision designed to save you blood, sweat, and tears.

My thought is that if you *do* find yourself caught in a battle with a bear over fish... **GIVE HIM THE FISH.**

It takes a strong person to stand up after losing a battle and regroup to get back in the fight. This is so vital to any new business start-up. Defeat is always sitting in the bushes, waiting for you to make a mistake, and when you do, it will be on you like white on rice.

Your one and only decision, when this happens, is this: do you stay and fight, or do you withdraw and let defeat have its fish?

Business is a tough gig and trying to win every battle is just not possible. You must make decisions about what you can and can't win. Learn from the mistakes that got you into the position of having to lose a battle and imprint it in your mind so that when a similar situation happens again, you can use your knowledge to avoid the same mistakes.

The battles will seem irrelevant once you have won the war, but it is those battles you lost just as much as the ones you won that will get you to where you want to be.

Endure More Pain Than Anyone Else

This is one of those topics that many people shy away from because they hate pain. I still allow myself to feel it. Procrastinator Me constantly gives me a quick stab in the gut when I see my ideas still undeveloped. It hurts me to think how well off I might have been had I stuck to my guns and followed through on one of those projects. I do not know for sure if success would have found me, but I can be sure I would have made a right royal go of it.

You must be prepared to accept the pain accompanied by the territory of operating a business, and you must be the one who stands up and hurts the most. People expect their leaders to lead, not sit on the sidelines sobbing because they lost their fish to a bear. You must be willing to bear the brunt of failure and show those who work for you that you can take it. Yes, it will hurt, and expressing this is allowed, but do not express it to the point of whingeing.

In any business, setting the pain of loss or setback is a tolerance that must be built up over time. Without it becoming a tolerance to you, it will hurt tenfold when it hits. Leaning into painful situations and problems will make you a better thinker, it will give you clearer direction and most of it will show you what not to do in the future.

As your tolerance for these types of painful situations arises—and they will arise—you must find yourself becoming more comfortable with the pain and more attuned with the need to find solutions. You will have a clearer understanding of the situation, and your focus will be centred on solving the issue instead of crying over it.

Yes, it will be difficult, it is pain after all, but you will learn to embrace it and you will learn to control its effects. Your view of it will change and it will cease to cloud your judgment and decision-making processes. If you are really good at it you will learn to capitalize on the pain.

Meetings are a prime example of somewhere that you can quickly learn to control pain (frustration and anger more often) and put yourself into an uncomfortable situation and not feel the effects of it. When someone says and persists on something that is contrary to your objectives, strategic goals or plans and will just not stop driving home their point you can refrain from blasting them back into last week.

I know that my personal de-stress activities are pretty weird, but they help me focus and reduce the stress I put on myself. Yes, they may be a bit weird to some, but I do them to release myself from the same activities I am doing which allows me to reset and go again:

- Write Fantasy Books
- Make Scratch build Models Spaceships
- Sitting outside and letting the cat attack my shoes (it's a cat thing)
- Grow vegetables (most of which I don't eat)
- Watch YouTube videos on how things work
- Play D&D

A great model I use for making sure my day is productive and not costing me time is called the Franklin Tri-Quation

Psychologist Nathaniel L. Branden, author of *The Psychology of Self-Esteem,* once pointed out the direct relationship between self-esteem and productive work. In essence, Branden observed that the better you feel about yourself, the more productive you will be; and the more productive you are, the better you will feel about yourself. I find this is true with me when I split up my time before I get frustrated and annoyed. Pushing through the pain is not always a great way to go. Sometimes you need to reset yourself and find the way you can be more productive and less destructive.

The productivity of the Franklin Tri-quation is shown below.

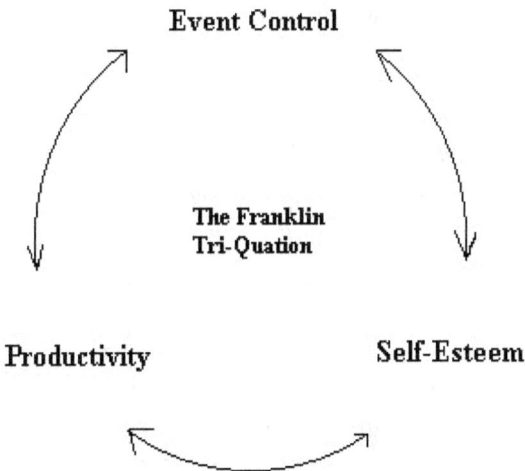

Event Control

The Franklin Tri-Quation

Productivity   **Self-Esteem**

Higher self-esteem raises productivity and event control. The easiest part of this tri-quation to attack is the event control piece. When you can control your own life, emotions and attitudes you can become more productive, better organised, and spend more time on activities that are of value. This includes your focus and mindset. The ultimate by-product of that is an increase your own self-worth.

1. Self Esteem = Productivity (High Producer = High Self Esteem, Low productivity = Low Productivity)

2. Event Control = How you handle your life and the events in a day will determine your productivity. Make a List of what you want to do and what you have to do and then priorities them.

3. Productivity = The level of what you achieve and what you are able to successfully complete. Achievement is a great way to feel positive. Try to achieve something every day; you will feel better, and your confidence will grow if you do.

James Ritchi once said a great way to grow yourself is to create a Personal Constitution. To me, this is a document that outlines your values and goals and establishes your mindset for going forward. It can put into perspective what you want to do and be most in life.

When you are willing to take the pain more so than anyone else to achieve your business make sure you do it with the right mindset. Ask yourself, what do you do in your daily tasks that will help you to my personal constitution, your goals.

If we get the mix right, then the pain we are willing to accept more than anyone else will not be so painful to us, and we will achieve more.

Starting with an Idea Hurts

When you start out with an idea, there is often a time when it hurts you to figure it out. You struggle with the Hows and Whys of it and then feel nauseous when you try to create it. You start out with such great enthusiasm and gusto that it's like success is just around the corner. However, it then hits you, the inevitable "Slacker Momentum", where you spend more time thinking about your idea instead of making it a reality. The laziness creeps in and begins to take over. Things become seemingly impossible, and you just want to go outside and play instead. This is where you must push yourself forward and make yourself stay on the road to success.

Do not fret, though. This happens to everyone. No one is born as a natural worker. We all have to push ourselves to become such. Hard workers are most often just people who have learnt to push themselves harder more often.

I think I am a hard worker. I work long hours so I can finish a job or project in plenty of time. I am almost always the last person to leave work and definitely the first to turn up. I will often find myself at work an hour early because it's quiet and no one bothers me. Right now, as I'm writing this, it is 1.35am: peaceful and quiet and much easier to work.

Below are some tactics you can apply to make yourself work harder. With enough practice, they may help you. Plus, a procrastinator needs all the help they can get.

Think about what it takes to fail, and then don't do that. If you understand what it will take to lose your goal, then you should be able to avoid it. Consider what it will be like to have people look at and comment on your failure. Don't give them the satisfaction.

Maintain a strong purpose and keep working towards it. Having a strong purpose can be a great way to keep yourself in check. If you have a simple goal like becoming financially free, then yes, you may one day achieve it, but if your purpose is to be financially free, rich, *and* live a life of luxury, then this gives you more of a purpose. Yes, you can settle for the lesser of the two, and I know many people say not to push too hard. But remember this: Normal work achieves a paycheck, but hard work achieves greatness.

Make sure you employ hard workers. They become your inspiration and motivation. As the boss, you must work hard but if your workers are working harder than you, then you must step up your efforts. Try not to get lost in the friendly aspect of employing people just so you can have fun. I'm not saying to not employ your friends (though you should be a little care with this), but I have seen too many friendships destroyed because of fights at work. Instead, find go-getters you can push and grow with. Healthy competition at work is a good thing and your staff will respect you more if they see you putting in the effort to try and work harder than them.

A great book on assuring you that you can achieve anything you want as long as you work hard is called

Success Through a Positive Mental Attitude by Napoleon Hill and Clement Stone. I learnt that your personal success, health, happiness, and wealth depend on how you make up your mind! It is your positive mental attitude that will make your life better. I encourage you to have a look at it. It's well worth the read.

It is difficult to endure more pain than everyone else when you don't believe in yourself or when you are pessimistic. However, being inspired makes you work harder to achieve your goals because being inspired make you believe in yourself just like when you walk out of an Avengers movie thinking you could be a superhero (you know you do).

Now this concept may be in direct conflict with some other points I make in this book, but my point is that working hard is just as important as working smart. Working hard nonstop is just plain crazy. Gary Vaynerchuk is an advocate of working hard and I love his take on the principle, but I also think that you can work hard to find ways to work smarter too. They go hand in hand.

By working harder than anyone else, you will know that your efforts will never be wasted as long as you keep working hard without giving up.

PART TWO

People Become Confident When They See You Are Too

As a business owner, there are certain elements of your being that should instil a sense of confidence and respect. People should know they can trust you and you, them.

As you develop a business, from the very outset you should be creating people that have confidence in you. Without confidence from those people, it will be hard to maintain a strong front and face the challenges that may come before you. For others to have confidence in you, there are some things you can do that will help to ensure they do.

First, you need to be willing to take the same risks in support of ideas and strategies, but do not under any circumstances take risks that put your integrity and honesty at risk. This is a sure-fire way to lose the respect quickly.

Be optimistic and positive, not just at work but out and about. Show people you are confident and alive. Staff tend to be attracted to optimism, which in turn brings with it more confidence.

"Positive thinking is powerful thinking. If you want happiness, fulfillment, success and inner peace, start thinking you have the power to achieve those things. Focus on the bright side of life and expect positive results."

Germany Kent

Be honest, no matter what. Honesty and integrity are key and should always be at the front of the decision-making processes. If people cannot trust you, they will not have confidence in you. Some decisions will be unpopular and have some ramifications but in the greater scheme of business, those inside your business and suppliers and customers outside will know that you are a person who can be trusted.

Learn from your mistakes and own up to your own failures. Do not be afraid of them. Embrace failure as an opportunity to learn. It's one thing to make a mistake, but if you never actually learn from it, then it was just a failure and a pointless exercise in stupidity. Staff do not take kindly to an incompetent boss, so be prepared to accept responsibility publicly for your mistakes on occasion. Some humble pie also helps to keep us level-headed and respectful of the process.

When people give you compliments, accept them graciously and do not, and I repeat do not, let them go to your head. This is again a sure-fire way to lose respect and confidence of your staff and outsiders.

One thing that I see often in business is where a business owner, especially those just starting out, begins to compare themself to others. This, more often than not, ends up in some form of negative perception about your lack of ability compared to this person or wish that you were able to do something like that person. This type of action is self-destructive not only for you but your staff. They should never see doubt in your eyes and fear or regret in your mannerisms.

Many people "fake it 'til they make it". I have done so in the past, and I sometimes need to fall back on it at times even today. But I have learnt to manage the situation to my advantage and only do it when I need to fill in a missing piece I have not yet had time to collect. I often say yes, I can do something, or yes, I can introduce you to people who can do this, simply because I know I can. I have used my life to build connections in most industries and have networks of people who I can connect with others, so when I say it, I know I can do it.

In front of people, your confidence in your own decisions and the strategic path you are taking will help you to embrace new ideas and create new opportunities out of necessity to not be left behind. Faking it is only as good as your ability to solve the problem for which your "faking it" was needed. If you cannot "make it", don't fake it.

Now, I am not talking about lying when I say this, but rather the situation where you may not have done something or may not have something available, so you say,

"Yes, I can do this" or "Yes, I can get this." If you don't have it or have never done it, but you know in your heart that you can, and you will then go for it, but tread lightly. It is a fine line between real capacity to deliver and flat-out incompetence and disappointment.

Teaching staff to focus and work on their strengths is important. They need to know that they are supported and that a failure is not a problem if they learn something from it.

"You don't hire for skills, you hire for attitude. You can always teach skills."

Simon Sinek

Self-confidence is a great tool to have and as a business owner you need to have this so that your staff will feel motivated. If you're motivated and confident then they will be too. It will take time to develop self-confidence in your employees, but the benefits are well work the hard work you will put in.

There are a few things you can do to build self-confidence in staff. Some of these work really well and can be taught quickly, while others will take more time:

Understand your employees' talents and help them to aim for their own goals. Give them the empowerment to become a manager if that is what they want to do. Help them develop a plan that will achieve this if it is possible. If not, then guide them in learning the skills they need. The objective is to encourage your staff to want to work for you because they see you have a vested interest in their success also.

Let staff share their skills with you. Staff often see what managers do not and they can be the greatest source of development and improvement in a company. As a manager, take time to get to know them and listen to their ideas. There are always great pearls of wisdom out there to be had. You just have to be willing to find them.

Give more authority to your staff. This is a big one and one that many owners and managers have a hard time doing. It means relinquishing some authority to someone who works for you. If you do, they feel more committed to doing better, and this can lead to stronger engagement with customers, better results, and improved performance.

Offer training and Professional Development. A big boost to a staff member is training, especially if that training is free. It shows that you value their efforts and are willing to invest in them and not just the business. Well trained workers also perform better as they can see improvements and make suggestions sooner because they know what they are looking for.

Meet with staff and have them participate in organizational changes and improvements. When you are a small close-knit team, getting your staff involved in major decisions, even if it is to listen to their advice and be a massive boost to their emotional state in the company.

They feel like part of the team and that their opinions matter.

Give praise when it due and encouragement when needed. People inherently like to be praised for their work. Giving praise when it's due instils positive feedback for the efforts and giving staff a positive outlook can help improve and instil even more confidence in them.

Ask for advice on matters that affect them. Sometimes, listening to ideas from people who are at the preverbal coalface can be very enlightening. Listening to these suggestions can often improve product performance or quality, reduce production times, and improve efficiency. Never be too proud to not take advice.

Help staff to learn from their mistakes. Understand that mistakes and accidents will happen. Be prepared for them, but don't lose it because they happen. If you are stable enough to accept some failures and accidents, then you should be stable enough to offer guidance and support. The staff member will be upset enough as it is. They don't need more negative comments from you, so avoid negative talk. As Yoda states, "This leads to the Dark Side."

Let staff members be part of the process of setting their own goals and KPIs. Getting staff involved in this is a great way to show commitment and fairness in the workplace. If they help to set their own targets, then they cannot complain about them. Help them by setting short, medium, and long-term goals. Together, you can find common ground, and this leads to a better relationship.

Sheep: When One Bleeps, They All Bleep So Tap into the Herd Mentality

People are like sheep. They will follow each other in a crowd simply to not be the one left out. They will buy the newest or latest phone or set of shoes because they don't want to be the one without it at the next get-together. This has always baffled me and continues to be something that I do not understand. See people will follow even if they do not understand what is happening.

I remember once, when I was teaching at Griffith University, I was asked to take an undergraduate lecture for a friend who was feeling sick. I had time for the course and didn't think anything of it. I did, however, have an idea that I had always wanted to try on a large group of students and thought this would be a great time to try it.

I mean, who doesn't want to mess with the minds of 380 fresh undergraduates?

I met with about six of the course students throughout the day of the lecture and set up my plan. I gave them clear instructions and then sent them on their way. They had been fed, were in on the plan, and went away totally oblivious to what I was going to do. All I had told them was that I needed you to follow my lead in the lectures. Whatever I do, you do." That was it.

The lecture was on Marketing Influence, and it was a perfect topic for the idea I had wanted to try for so long. I walked to the back door of Central Theatre 1 and stood there for a few seconds. Now, almost all lecturers would come in on the ground floor side door, so they don't have to walk up the stairs to the back door, but my plan involved no one knowing I was the lecturer.

I walked in and sat down about six rows down from the back and five seats in from the right side, and then I waited.

Within minutes, the theatre filled. I saw all six of the students walk, and in very poor attempts at disguise, they all looked at me wondering what I was doing seated with the students but then sat down anyway. Eventually, the theatre began to become quiet, and students waited for their teacher to arrive. Slowly, the noise began to rise as people drifted off into conversation with friends. Each small section of the room talks a little and a little more, trying to over-talk those around them.

I then struck.

First, I simply looked to one of my planted students, who sat right next to me and began to laugh very loudly. She, in turn, without hesitation, began to laugh at the same pitch I did, and within a split second later, the other five students did also. Now, I am sure they had told some of their friends to follow them and do the same things because within a split second later, another eight or so students around the theatre began to laugh as well. Slowly, as I laughed and the plants laughed, others began to laugh also.

More and more people joined in, so I stepped it up a notch. I stood up and pointed at the front of the room at the desk and laughed more and made WOW noises also. Without fail, my minion of plants did the same thing, and before long, almost every student was standing, laughing and pointing subconsciously, I bet trying to figure out what was going on but not wanting to be the one left seated.

My time was finally at hand. I laughed more and began to clap. Sure enough, within minutes, almost every student in the room was clapping and laughing, still making WOW sounds to the desk. I could not believe my eyes. My plan had worked and a hell of a lot better than what I had hoped.

I leant over to the young lady beside me and said to keep going. I then moved past the students and shot down the steps to the front of the room. I stood in front of the desk and took a bow as they applauded me and Wowed me. When they saw me arrive, it lasted about four seconds, but I will take it.

I waited till the room was silent and then stood there looking at them. Some were still giggling, some were wondering who I was, and some were on their phones texting. I then took a step forward, leaned a little further, and gave out a not-too-loud but loud enough "BAAAAAAAAA."

After the laughter died down, I explained my theory on herd mentality, which is that with some very minor influence or coaxing by people directed at the right people you can effectively make an entire crowd adopt a level of behaviour almost totally based on emotional reactions rather than rational thought and that these people would almost always make decisions differently in a crowd than they would had they been alone and given time to consider options.

When you want to create a need for a product or a desire to have it, you need to find a way to create a herd mentality. Get the big players or the influencers in a community to adopt, use, or promote your product or service, and if done correctly, the people will follow. See, no one wants to be left behind.

This type of behaviour is all around you every day. People are followers and don't want to stand out from the crowd, so they fall into line, literally at shops. For you, the decision on how creative you are in making large groups of people want your products or services is down to your imagination. Be the alpha sheep, and the rest will follow.

There is an author called Walt FJ Goodridge who describes the life of a sheep very well in one of his poems from a series he calls "Walt's Life Rhymes." I think it demonstrates the concept of following for the sake of following very well:

The Great Sheep Uprising

Walt's Life Rhyme #442

One day a young sheep woke

and faced a world he'd never known

He raced to tell the herd

and share the vision he'd been shown

The fence is down, the dog is dead

the shepherd's gone away!

We sheep will soon taste freedom

with no one to block our way!

What pastures shall we roam to?

Oh, what fields shall we explore?

Our day of choice has now drawn nigh

what greatness is in store?

We'll spread across the country!

Yes, expand our power base!

We'll maximize our numbers!

and reclaim our rightful place!

Imagine how we'll prosper

Yes, just think how far and wide

Our children spared enslavement

our own fate shall we decide

The sheep began to follow

with excitement this bold youth

But then an old sheep blocked their path

and spoke his only truth:

Contain your mad excitement

and now listen well, dear child

For sheep we are and sheep we'll be

and sheep do not run wild

Our master loved and led us

and this field is all we know

What lies beyond no one can say

this path may lead to woe

And so it was, that fateful day

the sheep fell back in line

No fence, no dog, no shepherd

just the limits on their minds

And so it is with sheep

And sadly so with us ourselves

That even blessed with freedom

all good sheep still herd themselves

The greatest challenge to being successful in business is not the economy, the market, your customers, or anything external. The single greatest obstacle you will ever face in turning your dreams into reality is overcoming the way you currently think. You have become herded into the mindset that you cannot change because change against the norm is not good for the greater good.

Your thoughts determine your beliefs, your beliefs set your expectations, your expectations influence your actions, and your actions create your reality. So, the first place to start in changing your reality, is to change your thoughts. Do not let the limitations for what society tell you be the defining principle on your choices. You be the principle. You make the decisions.

Human Capital. Surround Yourself with People Smarter Than You

This is my quotes section of the book. Below are just some of the greatest quotes I have come across and wish to share.

There was a man by the name of David Ogilvy, who is most notably known for being presented as the Father of modern advertising and is credited with saying *"If you ever find a man who is better than you are - hire him. If necessary, pay him more than you would pay yourself."*

There is also a reputed story of him giving each of his Directors at a directors meeting with a set of Russian dolls. When they opened the dolls, nothing seemed strange until they got to the smallest doll and opened it. Inside was a piece of folded paper on which Ogilvy had written, *"If you always hire people who are smaller than you, we shall become a company of dwarfs. If, on the other hand, you always hire people who are bigger than you, we shall become a company of giants."*

Henry Ford, who was once being questioned in a legal deposition, replied to a certain question and shocked the lawyer and most people in the room. His answer was the sign of an educated person. In reply to this particularly offensive question, he leaned over, pointed his finger at the lawyer who had asked the question, and said, *"If I should really WANT to answer the foolish question you have just asked, or any of the other questions you have been asking me, let me remind you that I have a row of electric push-buttons on my desk, and by pushing the right button, I can summon to my aid men who can answer ANY question I desire to ask concerning the business to which I am devoting most of my efforts. Now, will you kindly tell me, WHY I should clutter up my mind with general knowledge, for the purpose of being able to answer questions, when I have men around me who can supply any knowledge I require?"*

Alas, most of us must learn general knowledge when building up a business. One of the best books I ever read was the Autobiography of Andrew Carnegie. His passion for building an empire was simply awe inspiring yet his passion or helping others was just as inspiring and humbling.

Once, Napoleon Hill had an interview with Carnegie, hoping to find out the secret of his success and how he did what he did. Carnegie sat back in his study and looked calmly at Hill and replied that he could trace all of his knowledge and success to a single factor, "the sum total of the minds of his business associates–his managers, accountants, chemists, and so on. He referred to this combined brain power as a "master mind," and believed that he could state confidently that this was the power of his success.

If you have not done it, then try this: create your own Master Mind Group, or allow yourself to build up to one. Start with a focus group. I've done a number of them, and every time, I have come away learning more about myself and my directions. Sadly, the procrastinator in me has often managed to not act on advice when received that would have saved me from business pain.

This group should be allowed to present ideas for new products, services, or businesses with total respect and privacy. People in the group should expect and be willing to listen to constructive criticism, debate and discuss alternatives or variations and create and develop new ideas or changes to current ideas without ridicule or complaint.

As you develop these, you will begin to develop new and exciting possibilities and potential improvements to your own business idea or operations. A good group may give you suggestions, whereas a great group will give you inspiration and ideas.

Don't stifle the group, either. Let the ideas flow, the comments be expressed, and let the note-taking and creativity explode. Trust me when I tell you that these types of meetings are amazing and can really make a difference in how your own business moves forward, plus it's great free development knowledge. After all, aren't two heads better than one?

I have now formalized my focus groups and asked members to sign confidentiality forms. Ideas with direct business-changing potential are often pitched to my groups. This document also states that no ill feelings or actions are taken outside the group meetings.

When it comes to surrounding yourself with smarter people, you become smarter. If you employ them, they bring a culture and sense of imagination that may be lacking in you or your current team. Smart people spark creativity in everyone around them. They are smart and engaging, they inspire and uplift, and they listen to and are engaged in conversation and want to see change not just for themselves but for everyone around them. They potentially know things you can use that you may not have even thought of. Their understanding may just be the drop of wisdom that makes all the difference.

Here are some quick tips you can use to create your own focus group:

1. Do some research on who inspires you and reach out to them. With technology these days, they could be on the other side of the world and still be in the room at a meeting.

2. Use social media to its full advantage to get to know people you think would make a great addition to your focus group of business. Don't be afraid to reach out to anyone—what's the worst they can say to you? Social media like LinkedIn, Facebook, and Twitter are great places to connect to networks of smart and engaging people.

3. Go where smart people go. Free business events are excellent places as the people there are all the same as you, looking for inspiration and guidance. Just be careful not to sign up for too many courses or buy too many get-help packs.

4. Step out of your comfort zone and see what people have to say. Seek out comments on your plan. It's difficult and can be very uncomfortable, but it can also be very rewarding. Done right, it can change your perspective and lead you on a path to greatness.

5. Lastly, be engaging with everyone. Even the local postie can have useful insights, so get to know everyone around you. Introduce yourself and be open and engaging, and for the love of all things good, listen more than you talk. You have two ears, not two mouths.

You don't need to know everything, you just need to know where to find it or who to get it from.

Don't be Shy, Get out and Build Relationships

If you want to be in a business relationship with anyone – a client, vendor, or customer – how important is that relationship going to be to you? Will you value the relationship? Will you want to nurture it?

A business relationship, like any relationship, is a two-way street. The expectations of both parties need to be clear and easily understandable. Applying the Golden Rule is also a good idea:

"Do unto others as you would have them do unto you."

That is a very powerful statement, and one I try to practice in my daily life, both in business and personal matters. I also live by another thought that *Malcolm Gladwell* is known to have said which is *"Practise isn't the thing you do once you're good. It's the thing you do that makes you good."*

Good communication is key for any business relationship that you want to grow. Even when conflicts surface (and they will), keeping the lines of communication open at all times is extremely important. Meet conflicts head-on, no matter how frightening they may seem at the time. The sooner the issues are out on the table and dealt with, the sooner you can get back on track and back to business as usual.

Another thing to keep in mind is letting people know that you appreciate them. Thank-you emails, cards, and notes are always a good idea, and they never go out of style. People love to be appreciated. If you are receiving great business from someone, always be sure to let them know. You will feel better for it, and so will they. It may even lead to even more commerce together.

Another great idea is to reach out to your clients and customers on a regular basis by sending them monthly newsletters. This is a wonderful way to keep in touch, both to let them know you are thinking about them, and to remind them about you as well. Newsletters can be a tough task to try to develop and send, so be creative and use the talents of those around you.

Remember, you get out of a great relationship what you are willing to put into it. Value those you do business with. Nurture the relationships so they are always growing and prospering. Keep this up, and you will always have a garden full of healthy, happy business contacts.

Successful businesses know the importance of building and maintaining good working relationships, whether it is with partners, employees, business or trade organizations, the government, media representatives, vendors, consumers, or the community at large. A business must carefully balance the benefits of these interpersonal relationships and should never allow these relationships to blind their judgment, especially when it relates to what is in the best interest of the business's continued success and growth.

Buying advertising media based on interpersonal relationships is a common mistake made by many small businesses, especially when they are starting out. A Procrastinator will most likely throw the business's strategic marketing plan into the winds of chance in exchange for the warm and fuzzy feelings that come with doing business among friends. However, when the smoke clears, the business has made costly advertising expenditures with little or no results and the long-term negative effects may not readily be seen. Simply, the marketing/advertising expenditures have been made, the budget may or may not be busted, and the results may be none to little measurable penetration into your target demographic market segment.

Is buying media from a friend in the same industry always bad? Not always and maybe not ever; however, in order to choose the most effective media channels, you must first consider the audience or customer you are trying to reach. Developing a strong sense of the target demographics' buying and shopping patterns, interests and hobbies, entertainment, and media choices, for example, will lend itself a tremendous benefit to making informed media buying choices. Once you have developed a strong sense of what media channels may prove to be the most effective, you should try each a little at a time, carefully tracking the results. Once this is complete, you will be able to make an educated decision on where to invest your marketing dollars, prioritizing expenditures into the mediums that have proven results for your business.

Strong interpersonal relationships skills and the ability to develop and maintain good working relationships with a variety of people, businesses, and other organizations are imperative in today's business environments. However, the importance of a well-designed and implemented strategic marketing plan cannot be understated. It is paramount to the business's development and longevity, never taking second place to friendship.

It has been my experience that a successful business relationship is more often than not based on Value, Competence, Trust, and Propriety.

Value

Value: The customer's perception of your worth, excellence, usefulness, or importance. Value addresses the customer's question, "What can this person or company do for me?"

Value can be articulated by explicitly answering these questions throughout the sales cycle:

- How much? What can the customer expect to gain by doing business with you — in increased sales, lower costs, or something else?
- How soon? When will the customer be able to receive the value?

How sure? What will the proof be that the customer has indeed attained the value stated? Provide norms for the customer so that there is little question of what the customer can expect from you: "We have a track record of providing a 15% cost savings and 90% product availability within 2 days of order."

What are norms that your customers can expect you to live up to?

Remember, it is YOUR job to tell your customers what value they can expect — customers shouldn't have to work to figure out the value themselves. If you don't explicitly quantify the value your customer can expect to receive — and your competition may be doing this work for your customer — who is going to win the sale?

Competence

Competence: The customer's perception of your skill, knowledge, and experience with respect to them or their business. Competence addresses the customer's question, "Can this person or company do what they say they can do?"

Competence is demonstrated by the following:

- Completing and implementing an organized and logical sales approach
- Conveying an understanding of the customer and their business
- Demonstrating research and knowledge

- Substantiating your capabilities

Involving team members appropriately and on a timely basis. The perception of competence is gained over time. As you work these guidelines into your approach to your customers, you will gain credibility and enhance your business relationships.

Trust

Trust: The customer's confidence in your integrity, ability, and intent. Trust addresses the customer's question, "Do I trust this person?"

Trust is demonstrated by the following:

- Using third-party introductions
- Providing a letter of recommendation (objective references help build credibility)
- Displaying honesty, candour, empathy, and respect (show that you've done your homework; show concern for their time and issues)
- Conveying win/win intent (concern for positive outcome and success for both parties)
- Above all else, substantiate with each action:
- A track record of follow-through

o New norms or guidelines for expected behaviour that are agreed to and can be counted on.

Propriety

Propriety: The customer's perception of the appropriateness or properness of your actions with respect to them or their business. Propriety addresses the customer's question, "Is this person behaving properly or appropriately?"

Part of exhibiting propriety is in the way you present yourself. Over half of others' perceptions of you are based — at least initially — on your appearance. Therefore, take care in your physical appearance, mannerisms, vocabulary, and business etiquette. If your first "appearances" occur on the phone, pay special attention to your tone, enthusiasm, and vocabulary.

A second, critical part of demonstrating propriety involves your adaptability to other people. In business, the Golden Rule — "Do unto others as you would have them do unto you" — is usually inappropriate. In fact, if you treat others as you want to be treated, you may end up ignoring their needs, wants, and expectations, which may be completely different from your own.

You must be astute enough to recognize others' needs, wants, and expectations AND you must be flexible enough to treat people the way they want to be treated. Relate to your customers in a way that makes them feel most comfortable. This decreases relationship tension and increases trust, credibility, cooperation, and the commitment to work with you.

Build your business relationships — and your future — by focusing on the critical elements of Value, Competence, Trust, and Propriety.

Don't Pigeonhole Your Workers

When you employ someone, what are you employing? Are you employing their talents, experience, personality, or a mixture? If asked, most would say it was a mixture. This is important because this is where hidden talent may be, and it often goes unnoticed because employers forget to utilize all of what they say they employ.

We tend to have the weird habit of forming an opinion of people at first site or establishing a perception of someone after a short period of time, especially when we do not work directly with someone in the business. We base our thoughts and comments on them from what we may read in their progress reports and **KPI** (key performance indicator) results.

I say this with true belief and in the hope that I do not offend, but I believe that the days of fair and equitable opportunity in the workplace are here and that, while still growing, the opportunity for employers to take advantage of everyone under their employ is now.

Sadly, though many form opinions of people for a variety of reasons, this can cloud judgment and create resistance toward them despite the possible evidence that the person may have matured or developed a stronger set of talents.

I remember once when I consulted with a company that had over 40 salespeople across the country, all with varying qualifications, experience, and knowledge of the products and their industry. It was an interesting experience visiting with many of them in Brisbane once and being able to hear how they worked and what drove them. Something, however, stood out to me that I could not wave off. They all seemed to be working under the same premise that there was only one way they could work and develop new clients. It struck me as odd because the CEO was such a relaxed and idea-driven person. Surely, these people could develop different strategies and create innovative methods for sales development.

And then I met the COO. What a tool.

This person in a position of extreme influence and power over the entire business decided that his methods of operational growth were the only way to move a company forward and had made everyone use his approach to growth. In essence, they had pigeonholed the entire company into one group mindset, and the company paid the price. They were operating above the line and making some money, but nothing like what they had the potential to make. In fact, they were far from it.

Now, I do not like to get people fired, but I can tell you I quickly got my facts together and presented them to the CEO, who was also the owner. It became apparent to him very quickly that this person was dragging the company down. The problem was that this person could not just be fired. Strict laws prohibited this from occurring, so they were here for the time being. I had a feeling that change and certainly changes to their procedures would not be taken to happily.

A meeting was held where I was simply an observer, and I watched as the CEO explained to the COO that the salesforce should have the ability to develop leads, create opportunities, and look at new ideas in their own individual capacity. The CEO went on to explain that things needed to be pushed along and some fires should be lit under some of the more mature salespeople (that was my line). Also effectively immediately, a new sales manager would be brought in to manage the salespeople because the CEO felt that the COO needed support in an ever-growing business sales force (this was a bit of a white lie from the CEO I did not see coming, but it sure worked). The COO did not take kindly to this and saw it as an undermining of their authority instead of an opportunity to expand new horizons and be creative. Within several hours, their resignation was on the CEO's desk. It was at that time in my career that I realised that things in the movies actually do happen in real life.

Needless to say, the company went on to grow and expand internationally and grow to a diverse and ideas driven business that eventually was sold for a sum far greater than I think the owner ever expected.

When we force people to resign themselves to being pigeonholed because of the way we treat them, we end up losing a lot of their abilities and potential. We fail to see the true capacity of someone and miss out on the potential they have, and this can be an expensive learning experience for a business. This is often a major factor in businesses with high turnover. People do not like to be stifled if they are creative thinkers. They should be allowed to explore opportunities to hole grow the business.

Of course, there are tasks and requirements that need consistency and an unwavering process to be followed, but you should not look at this as a bad thing. It is part of the process of running a business. However, you should consider the people you are doing this to and understand that they may have some ideas on innovation and development also. So, take the time to hear from them even if they may not work in the innovative and idea-driven sector of the business.

It is hard not to pigeonhole people, especially when you have a goal and strategy planned out. Perseverance involves change and being open to ideas. Struggles will occur, mark my words, but like I have said previously, if you surround yourself with smart people, let them be smart for you. Do not stifle the smarts you so eagerly pay for. Use it, groom it, and let it fly.

Just in a few final points on Sales and teaching people how to sell. People like to hear a story. They associate their own life if they can relate to what you are saying easier. It is often difficult to connect with a customer if you cannot form a sort of "bond" with them. Finding common ground is a challenge, and so I use a few terms when I am talking with people.

I call it the RPK method of Building Customer Rapport. So, let me explain. RPK stands for:

I Remember

I Promise

I Know

"I Remember" = This is where you relate a story to them that their subconscious can attach itself to, and they can form a connection to what you are saying. As an example, let us say you want to sell a family van, "I remember the time I was with my family, and we had just bought a new van like this one. Man, the feeling of being able to spread out and relax meant the kids did not play up so much. It made outings so much more enjoyable. I am not saying to lie but you should have plenty of experiences in your life of the products you are trying to sell that you can reflect on and use.

"I Promise" = Yes, I know, "Don't promise something you can't deliver", right? Absolutely correct. Make sure you can fulfill the promise. This is a must. Your reputation and future integrity are on the line. Your team should know what they can and cannot deliver. A strong commitment like this can be the lynchpin in a deal, but delivery goes hand in hand so make sure your promise is achievable.

"I Know" = You must have confidence in your own products and services. Your team must have the same confidence. They need to be able to say with complete confidence and utter conviction that they know the product or service will meet the needs and requirements of the person they are talking to. Every customer wants reassurance and confidence. Think about how many times you have gone into a store and asked which product is best, and the salesperson says, "I like this one, I have this at home, and I love it."

Your staff are so important so make sure you give them the tools they need. Sales is a vital part of the process so a few extra tips can help them achieve.

Shut Up, Watch, and Listen

One of the hardest lessons I have ever had to learn, and one that I still sometimes find the hardest, is to shut up and listen. Though I have gotten much better at it over time, I am a talker. I like to talk. I enjoy stringing words together. I know words, and when I am forced to listen more, I find myself becoming fidgety.

It is amazing what you can actually learn when you just listen. People divulge information quite readily if you take the time to hear what they are saying. It is amazing how much you can tell from someone just by the way they talk and what they do.

I used to work on the third floor of The Mansions building at 40 George Street in Brisbane. It was built in 1889, and it is a beautiful building and I still love it more than anywhere I have ever worked.

There was a cat sculpture outside my window, which I had named Doug, and every morning, I would say hi to it when I sat down at my desk. I had a great fondness for the cat, not because of what it was but because it had a great view of the street below, as did I. I could see people coming and going from some of the most influential buildings in Brisbane at the time, there were there a lot of people moving around. This is where I think I began my journey into watching people. I mean, really watching them.

I would often go downstairs and walk along the street to the mall, just sitting and watching people going about their business. I thought about who I saw and how often I saw them. I remember several people who I saw fairly regularly, and over time, I felt I got to know them a little personally even though I never actually met them.

One person stands out the most, as she was always bright and happy and walked with purpose. Her smile was inspiring, and her attitude was almost contagious. Over a period of several months, though, I began to notice little changes. Less attention to her dress or her hair not done up the way she would normally do it. Even to the point that slip-ons replaced her high heels. Then one day, I saw her walking with a sombre demeanour and almost pain. She looked like you would think someone would look if they had heard news of such profound sadness that it completely engulfs them. Something had happened to this lady that had completely changed the way she was. I never knew what happened, but I think of the change I saw happen to this person often, and it reminds me of taking notice of people I work with and watching for subtle changes in them so that I might be able to help solve any issues that cause changes like I saw in this lady.

You can learn a great deal from listening more than speaking. People's pitches to you are often just the covering they use to disguise their true plan underneath. If you are a person of influence, they often hide what they really want to say as a way to avoid disappointment from you or their boss. This is where the great skill in listening closely comes into play. This is where you are a boss, an employer as a fellow worker can make or break a person if you are not observant enough.

What you don't hear in someone's pitch to you can be more powerful than anything said verbally. If you know to listen for what is not being said, then you can better understand the strategy you need to follow.

"That's it. The explanation is simple, but the development and execution of a strategy are by no means simplistic."

Art Petty

Knowledge can be a powerful ally and with that power comes great responsibility to use it wisely. People feel like they have been listened to if you speak less and listen more. It also creates a sort of reverse influence experience for you in as much as that when you speak, people will stop and listen to you also.

Be an active listener first. This means taking part in a conversation and developing a relationship with the person you are speaking with. Listen to them, understand them by showing your interest. Do not wave off their ideas as folly. Be willing to give them enough of your time so they feel empowered by you. Give them a sense of accomplishment.

People like Stephen Covey have a great chapter in his book, *The 7 Habits of Highly Effective People,* that you should read all about listening. I'm not going to spoil it for you, but trust me — if this is an area you need help with, then grab that book.

Finally, it all boils down to how much you want to be listened to also. If you listen to your employees and those people around you, then you will learn so much more than you thought. There is a world of information out there in the minds of great people that you should aim to grab and work with. They will give so much more in return if they know they are being listened to.

You can build an entire business on this alone. Great businesses have flourished simply by creating environments where innovation and ideas are encouraged and nourished. This can be your business too if you do it right.

You Are the Leader, so you need to Step Up

As a business owner, you are a leader. With that title comes a level of responsibility that you must know and understand before going in. It is vital to be aware that the title of leader, manager, boss, and owner are inherent with a queasy sense of power that people will adhere to. Even the shyest and most timid of people if in a position of authority will be afforded that authority by people under them.

As a business procrastinator, I have attended so many workshops, seminars, and events on being a great leader or becoming a public speaker that I can almost recite some of their speeches word for word. Most of the stuff you read these days has been regurgitated so much that it is often impossible to really understand where or from whom it first came from.

But there are some slivers of truth and knowledge I have gleaned from these business gurus that I find helpful for new business owners. Most talk about them as if they are golden drops of wisdom they want to pass on to you that they have found, almost like they are precious revelations that only they seem to know about and now want to share with you in their special training program or introductory plan. But really, they are common sense practices that anyone with a sense of decency and respect for themselves and others should know.

That being said, I am going to share with you what I think are the stand-out ones. Now, I have been asked if I call them anything, some fancy list or amazing set of skills. I simply call them "Being a Good Person" rules. It's a list of things I have found that seem to be universal traits in all good leaders.

- Integrity is paramount to everything
- A positive and passionate attitude can move mountains
- Actions often speak louder than words
- Forgiveness is a two-way street in business
- Pay attention to everyone
- Be humble enough to ask for help
- Show confidence always

- Communicate often and respect always
- Work for your staff, not the other way around
- Be creative

Being a good leader is important. A moral leader provides value or meaning for people to live by and be inspired by. It gives them inspiration to act and motivation to hold themself accountable. As a leader, it is your responsibility to be good at leading. It is not someone else's responsibility to tell you how to lead. Being a leader has power that should not be taken for granted.

"If you have some power, then your job is to empower somebody else."

Toni Morrison

Working to be the best of yourself, the best leader you can be is tough, don't get me wrong, but it is essential if you do not want your business to fail. Some points to remember when striving for great leadership, because great is what you should be striving for, are:

1. Have values others can see in you and stick to them.

Good leaders use their morals and values to give guidance to their own lives first. Then be the example of these values to your team. Hard work, respect, honesty, and integrity are all the values that a good leader should have and use. And don't forget to be fair. This is a big one because this is where staff will form opinions about you and how you treat others.

2. If you have an ego, shelve it or lock it away. There is no room for it.

You need to have a sense of yourself and should not be threatened by others. You are not the most important thing in the business. A true leader is not about being the Top Dog. It is about being there for others and serving them. Leave your personal interests at home when you are leading. Focus on those who work for you and make sure that you put the interests of others first.

3. Look at the diversity of your team and use their skills and knowledge to complement your own.

People have all sorts of diversity and values that make up the workforce. You should not force your values on others but rather consider other people's values. Be a leader who interacts with others and understands them. This is a great way to build trust, and the combination of collective values of diverse groups informs and develops long-term goals better and with more clarity. A good leader should not be afraid to change when needed and should actively seek out leadership qualities in their workforce, as this helps everyone to align their convictions and achieve the objectives of the company.

4.   Be one with the group. Be one with the team.

I can assure you that it will be almost impossible to have everyone on board all the time. In fact, I dare say that it will be impossible to do so, but you should be willing to listen to everyone no matter what their point of view is. Don't try to win everyone over to your side. A bit of diversity is a good thing as it helps bring a different perspective to the discussion.

5.   Be known as THE COMMUNICATOR.

Just like The Terminator, when you say you will be back, mean it. Don't talk for the sake of talking. A great leader does their best to communicate with staff as often as they can. You should really mean it when you say you want to hear their ideas. Have a strong purpose that can inspire action and growth because people want to take part in creating a positive change. Really listen to them when they ask to be heard.

The greatest leaders in history were the ones who had the ability to command the respect of the people who followed them. This is something that they earned. It was not blindly given to them. One can be given authority by simply being in a position. However, no position can garner respect. It is the actions of the individual that lead to others providing it.

Leadership hinges on how you work with other people. Just as it pays to know your own strengths and vulnerabilities, it is also important to understand what motivates people to work with you. Simon Sinek is a British-born American author and motivational speaker. He is the author of five books, including *Start With Why* and *The Infinite Game*, and he states that you have two choices: you can either influence human behaviour through manipulation or inspiration.

I remember being in the army reserves and speaking to a Warrant Officer about why he had been in the army so long but never risen above the rank they were at. He told me that people respected him for his knowledge and respected him for his wisdom. He liked the feeling this gave him, and becoming an officer may have diminished this feeling for him. He went on to explain that many officers, especially young Lieutenants, were under 25 and fresh out of military college. They had earned their rank, not through years of training and combat but through study and practice, and he was worried if he became one that, people would not give him the same respect he now had.

I could understand the rationale he was using, but I also thought it was an odd way to look at the dedication of someone who had studied hard and worked to achieve the result. I think he was a bit set in his ways because I would often hear him say, "Respect the rank, but you don't have to respect the person." This was a statement I heard over the years from several ranked personnel, and while I understood what it meant, I also did not think it a good mantra to have. I found that respecting everyone, irrespective of rank or level of knowledge, was a far more accepting approach, and it never let me down.

One of the most basic ways to gain the respect of those with whom you work is to be an example. Whatever you preach, be certain that you are living it. Leadership and management are not about issuing orders. It is about making decisions that are to the benefit of the business. Sometimes, these decisions may come in conflict with the "troops." How these challenges are surmounted is partially contingent upon the respect you have from the people who work for you.

"The main difference between the two is that leadership is about influencing people to follow, while management focuses on maintaining systems and purposes."

John C. Maxwell

It seems that a lot of people in authority will work with the attitude "Do as I say, not as I do." This is a surefire way to instil resentment among those you are meant to be leading. They will begin to question why they should do something that you are not willing to do. There is a lot to think of in this simple statement. How can you expect someone else to do what you are not willing to do yourself? In any business setting, this is a misguided way to run a business.

Leading through your actions is one effective way to gain the respect of your staff. Another is to exemplify the characteristics that the organisation is promoting. If you are seeking honesty, a willingness to work, and intelligence, it is best to have these traits yourself. People are more apt to stay and work late if they see you putting the hours in also.

Similarly, if you are willing to "get your hands dirty", the staff will see it and realise you are not looking down at them. Businesses make the lines of command clear. A leader who is a working part of them team will have the respect of those in the team.

Another great experience I had in the Army Reserves was when I was challenged on a live firing range. I was being trained as a Range Safety Officer and it was my responsibility to ensure all safety procedures were followed, no questions asked. No one stepped onto the "mound" unless authorized by me to do so, especially when live firing was taking place. As far as anyone was concerned, the Range Safety Officer was God.

Back then, we spoke pretty rough, and while I did not swear, I could raise my voice just as loud as anyone and be quite intimidating if I had to. On one shift, I was completing a practice class with a group of 12 new recruits. All stations were full, and all weapons were hot (meaning safety was off) when I noticed a rover pull into the parking area. Two people got out and walked towards the mound. I instantly began to keep an eye on them as I had no idea who they were, and I had not received any notice of additional soldiers being on site.

After about 15 minutes, I found myself down the far end of the firing line, and I could see two of the men begin to walk up onto the mound. I immediately halted fire and yelled out to the two men approaching the first firing position. "What the hell are you doing? Get the hell off my mound, are you an idiot?" I said, storming towards them. By this time, my supervisor had taken notice, and I could see him standing on the bottom of the mound, watching.

As I approached, I saw that it was a Major and a Captain. Deep down inside, in places I don't like to go, I thought my career in the army had just ended. "I am Major Dumbass (last name protected for privacy) and blah blah blah." I don't remember exactly what he said, but it was something about him needing to do his fire practice today, and at one point, Captain Nobs (again, a fake name for privacy) piped in, yelling also. I stood there and let them have their little rant. See, I had been taught about authority and leadership from the man at the bottom of the mound, who had still not stepped one foot up even when all the yelling began.

After some time of attempting to intimidate me and threaten me, the officers turned to my Sergeant and demanded I be escorted off the mound and charged with insubordination. Sergeant Hero (yep, he was) ignored them and asked me for permission to come onto the mound. I nodded and he walked up and gave these two the best dressing down I had ever heard. He used terms like authority, safety, compliance, idiot, instruction, manners, respect, command, and a bunch of other words I cannot write, so fast that these two officers did not know what to do. They looked at him, then at me, then back at him, and walked off. Sergeant Hero gave me a nod, then turned and walked off the mound behind them like he had just come up to give me a drink of water.

Another way to gain respect is to keep the lines of distinction clear. Too often, owners become friends with those whom they are leading, and while this is not necessarily a bad thing, it can create situations where a mixture of emotions can come into play. Leading involves making decisions. Unfortunately, it is impossible to keep everyone in an organisation happy all the time. There will be some who feel that a particular choice negatively affects them. In those instances, if there is a "friendship" between you and your staff, some will take it personally. In a healthy managerial position, your staff will realise that your selections are based upon what is best for the company without regard to personal likes.

The example you set is the one that will filter through your team. In the era of rapid change, one of the qualities needed is the ability to learn. When people work for a leader who falls behind in terms of advancements, their respect dwindles. I once was in a situation where I consulted for a business owner who had no idea what their business was about, and to top it off, she did nothing to improve her level of understanding. She was a great person, and her business was excellent, but it was run by everyone but her. She sat at her desk but didn't really do or achieve anything. Even after months of trying to train and guide her, she was still as bad as she was. Her interest in the business was money, so that is all she was interested in: getting her coin at the end of each week was substantial enough. She had the authority of ownership, and with that position came what she thought was the power to do whatever she wanted. However, she did not have the respect of anyone on our team.

The days of operating in an "ivory tower" are history. People are too transient to work under such conditions. By the time individuals reach their mid-30's, they have worked under a variety of different managers, owners and leaders. This gives them a wide scope of experience. If you can curry their respect, the chances of retaining them are greatly increased.

Let it all hang out. Know How to Motivate

They say you can lead a horse to water, but you cannot make it drink. Well, for that matter, you can't make it eat, stand, roll over, or walk a plank. Maybe the horse was not thirsty, or maybe the horse had a bad experience the last time it was led to water. Who knows, but in the business world, motivation is everything. This is a key part of what a procrastinator lives. Motivation. They want to do everything. They want to have people feel the joy of success with them, and they want to feel the sweet, sweet joy of standing in front of the world and saying, "I MADE IT." But alas, this is more than likely not happening or may never happen. Why? Because they had forgotten to motivate not only the people around them but also themselves.

When it comes to motivation, a true procrastinator will lay in bed at night and think of the success they will achieve by putting into action certain plans, strategies, and procedures. They will think about opportunities and ideas that are sure to be the key to everything and, while still with their head on the pillow, begin to calculate the money that will roll in. This is the life of a serial procrastinator. See, the following morning, they will go back to doing the same thing they always do, and then that night, they will go through the same routine of thoughts again. They are motivated in their own mind, but in reality, they are as lacklustre as any person waiting for a bus in the rain. Uncomfortable, stressed, and not quite sure why they just didn't take the train.

Knowing how to motivate is a big deal. I mean, really motivate, inspire, and empower. But do we do it? The simple answer is no. You, like me, have been or still are the quintessential pillow motivator. You give yourself all the confidence and motivation in the world, only to fall asleep and relive Groundhog Day again.

Great companies don't hire skilled people and motivate them. They hire already motivated people and inspire them.

"People are either motivated or they are not. Unless you give motivated people something to believe in, something bigger than their job to work toward, they will motivate

themselves to find a new job and you'll be stuck with whoever's left."

Simon Sinek

Again, an overused statement is "Where there is no will, there is no way." This also is rubbish. There is *always* a way. It's just that most people are not looking at the situation in the right way. They need to look at the problem or situation to help them find the drive they need to take the necessary steps to change the situation. Once you or the people you work for find the drive and master the motivation they need, then there is nothing that can hold them back.

I have learnt and taught the simple rule of Why and How.

The Why represents all the reasons I need to do something, or the reason I want someone else to do something. It is the persona of the proposition your mind needs to justify the actions you will take to make the situation become a reality in the manner you need it to. Even you need to understand that.

"A well-known principle of human behavior says that when we ask someone to do us a favor we will be more

successful if we provide a reason. People simply like to have reasons for what they do."

Robert Cialdini

More often than not, we do things in business for the wrong reasons. Ask yourself this: do you complete a task because it has to be done, or are you trying to complete it so you can learn something new? You may even be doing it because you don't know any other way to get it done. If this is the case, then there is a problem with your Why. You should always know exactly why you do something and what benefit it will have on the overall success or outcome you are aiming for. If you can't say the Why to an action, then stop doing it and do something productive.

This leads into the How. A good example of the How is when you need to get something done quickly because you failed to get it done sooner. University students have amazing Hows when they need to. They know they have an assignment due on XYZ date, yet leave it until the last possible minute to get it done, and still manage to hand in an assignment. Their Why never changes, they do it because it's part of their course, but their How changes dramatically.

This Why and How method can work on motivating people, including yourself. Why do you want to do what you want to do, and how are you going to do it? The motivation part comes at the end when you see what you are aiming for. The results are the actual Why. The How becomes the vehicle in which you drive to achieve it.

Motivating people to succeed and achieve desired results requires you to understand their Why and How. You have some leverage on these, but a good boss gives guidance and direction in what needs to be done and then allows the staff to determine the Why and How. With most business relationships with staff, money is a major motivator.

A good manager or owner will work with their staff to achieve their goals. They will encourage creativity and expression instead of stifling it. They will show empathy when things do not go right or when a failure is the result of something. They will be motivated through actions and allow staff to follow those actions in return. You become the boss who helps their staff to understand that they are choosing to do this or that for you because they have seen the motivation you are willing to give them, and they like it.

If you can get your staff or even your own self to choose to do something rather than having to do something, then you stand a far better chance of success.

Some ways that you can create the motivation of choosing to do something or wanting to succeed are simple and not at all hard. If your motivation is purely for money's sake, then you will most likely never succeed to the level you are hoping. Sure, you will make some money, but your real Why will continue to go unachieved, and you will fall into the procrastinator's world of great dreams and great ideas but no substance.

There is no particular set of rules that one should follow in motivating employees. We each have our own driving force when it comes to doing an excellent job at work. A working mother could be motivated by her children, who serve as her inspiration to succeed. A trainee who is fresh out of college is motivated by the compulsion to learn and climb to the top. A long-time company employee will get motivated to perform well so that they can be promoted. Others are motivated by financial rewards. As a business owner, you need to determine the individual driving forces of those who are on your team so that you can create a motivated workforce. They will be your strength and the ones you will need to lean on to support you going forward.

1. Goals for Employee Motivation:

- Increase employee performance at work
- Spice up team spirit and build a cohesive team
- Eliminate individual differences and avoid conflicts
- Have an open communication between peers
- Set and achieve a common goal

2. Lead by Example

There is one joke that says that the new definition of a boss is one who is always early when you are late and who is always late when you are not. Do not let this apply to you. Be consistent. The simple gesture of arriving before or at the same time as your employees will show them how much you value their time and yours. This is also a good way of showing employees that you respect the company that pays you for your time at work. If you do come in late, apologize to those who are under you and explain why you are late. This is so that they will not think that the no-late policy does not apply to the boss, showing them that you are equals when it comes to company rules and policies.

"The three most important ways to lead people are: by example… by example… by example."

Albert Schweitzer

3. Keep Communication Lines Open

Some employees are afraid to talk to or even look at superiors who exude the touch-me-not aura. This is not a good way to motivate your employees. When you come to work, do not just go straight to your office and deal with your paperwork. Mingle with the employees and ask them about their day and what they have accomplished so far. Then you can tell them about the output that you expect by the end of the day. This way, you will know what to expect from the employees and vice-versa. It will not only help you set a goal for the day, but with this, you are also optimizing your interaction with the employees by mingling with them on a more casual basis.

4. Share What You Know

Do not be selfish with what you know. Sometimes, a business does not grow because there are employees who know something advanced about the industry or a certain aspect of the company, and they are not willing to share their knowledge with others. They think that this would make them invaluable to the company, especially if they are the only ones who know about a particular process or idea. This attitude would not help your company succeed.

There should always be a sharing of knowledge from both directions. When an employee is asked to train abroad, they are often asked to sign a contract that they should not resign for the next year or two. Why do you think this is so? Imagine what would happen if the employee who trained abroad or attended an exclusive seminar about advanced technology in the industry just up and left right after the training, and trust me, it happens. I have seen this firsthand once by not listening and taking some advice I offered about contracts. It was a devastating end result for the company.

A company will not spend thousands of dollars to train an employee for nothing. They want you to share and impart the knowledge to your fellow employees. If you share a new technology with your entire team, who knows what newer and better ideas the knowledge would bring? Do not stunt the company's growth by keeping your ideas to yourself.

5. Implement Your Ideas

What good would a new idea or technology do if you do not apply it? After sharing the knowledge, gather the team and think of ways to improve the company's operation with what you all have learned. As a leader, you should be a people person. You must know how to adapt to the things that motivate your team members and use this knowledge to your advantage. Without a good and solid workforce behind you, you will not accomplish anything. You may have ten or a hundred employees, but if you apply these steps to motivate your team, you can bring out the best in them and contribute towards your company's growth and success.

PART THREE

Work Smarter Not Harder is a Lazy Person's Shortcut.

Author Roy Primm wrote:

Getting more done with less is an art,

It's a quality requiring much heart,

But I must confess

How I turned failure to success

Was to work both hard and work smart.

I've heard two schools of thought when it comes to achieving maximum success in a minimum amount of time. The first school is to work hard, long hours, nose to the grindstone, and burning the midnight oil. I've heard many people say that is the only sure way to achieve lasting success. I previously mentioned that famous influence Gary Vaynerchuk is an advocate of this style of success. While I love his messages and think he is an amazing person to study, I am not sure if I think this method is for everyone — especially those who have the know-how and capacity to do it smarter.

But I am sure you know many people who have worked hard for years and have yet to achieve what most people would call success. In fact, you may be one of them. I was one of those people. I discovered many years ago that hard work alone is not a guarantee of success. If it was, you'd see more millionaires.

The other school of thought says to work smart, not hard. The work smart philosophy says, "Less is better." Delegate and use other people's time, money, and hands as much as you can. They say this is the quickest way to success.

With so much talk about working smart, many people, especially those new to running a business and young people, are starting to get the impression that good old-fashioned hard work went out with the horse and buggy. They feel hard work is no longer required to achieve success. After all, we now have computers, e-mail, and cell phones.

I must admit they both have their benefits and their limits. Through experience, I've discovered that the best way to achieve maximum success in a minimum of time is to work hard at working smart!

Yes, working hard at working smart will give you the best of both worlds without the limits each one has by itself. When you work hard at working smart, you're maximizing your potential to the fullest. You have your pedal to the metal, and you're going full speed ahead - but you're doing it in the most efficient way possible.

Here are seven quick and easy ways to help you work hard at working smart every day. If you take the time to make these tips a habit, you'll find yourself achieving your goals much quicker.

1. Work hard at being more adaptable to changes.

Remember that every change that comes your way gives you an opportunity to move ahead of those who won't or can't adapt to sudden change. In life, they say the only guarantees are death and taxes. I would like to add a third item, and that is CHANGE. Try to be the first to learn and adapt to new changes in your industry, in new technologies, and in new techniques.

"A wise man will make more opportunities than he finds."

THE BUSINESS PROCRASTINATOR

Francis Bacon

2. Work hard at looking for shortcuts in everything you do.

Always be alert to easier, more efficient ways of doing your routine tasks. Can you cut out, reduce, speed up, or combine steps without sacrificing effectiveness? Don't fall into the habit of doing routine tasks with a routine attitude. Stay alert to the possibility of doing it in a different way. Think outside the box if it can save you time, money, or frustration.

3. Work hard at thinking ahead as much as possible.

The best chess players always think one move ahead. You should try to do the same. Prepare yourself mentally before you act physically. This alone will help you avoid wasting time and making costly mistakes. The best athletes establish the habit of anticipating their next move ahead of time. The best quarterbacks know what they'll do if their primary receiver falls down.

4. Work hard at finding working hard at working smart role models.

Always be on the lookout for people who work hard at working smart. Here's a hint: they'll usually be the people who do more in less time and with fewer sources of money, time, or people to help them than others.

5. Work hard at learning quickly from your mistakes and the mistakes of others.

You're smart if you can learn from your mistakes, and you're intelligent if you can learn from others' mistakes — but you're wise if you can do both. Learn how to fail constructively. You learn constructively when you ask who, what, when, why, and how questions. For example, next time, who will I consult with first? What did I do wrong? When did I do it? Why did I do it, and how can I do better next time?

6. Work hard at finding ways to multi-task wisely.

What's most important about multitasking is knowing when to multitask and when not to. Routine tasks are perfect for multitasking. But detailed, risky, and dangerous projects should not be.

7. Work hard at keeping current on the latest technology related to your task.

Allow technology to help you work harder at working smarter. Whatever your task, there is a gadget, software program, or tool that can help you do it more efficiently.

It is my hope that these seven tips will inspire you to think of more ways you can work hard at working smart. The benefits and satisfaction will be well worth your time and effort.

Running a business can often stretch you to the limit, so to be effective at doing what you do best, it's imperative to look at what tasks you can either delegate or outsource.

Delegating

This is an interesting word. For some people, it means completely letting go of their responsibilities and getting someone else to do the work. Now that's all well and good, providing that you train that person on how you've been handling those tasks. Show them how it's been done first.

For many business owners and managers, delegating means completely abdicating all responsibility for a particular task to somebody else without showing them how. They expect that person to know how to do it immediately.

Well, forget it. No wonder you often hear people say, "I tried to delegate that task, but no one was as good as me at doing it!" or, "I just couldn't find the right person who was capable of taking on those responsibilities."

That's an interesting comment. Often people are given responsibilities for which they have had no training in and are then expected to know how to carry out those duties. A great example of this is when a person is promoted to manager/team leader, and they are automatically expected to know how to manage themselves and their people.

Coming in From the Outside

How about the new kid on the block who comes in to take up the reins in a position that has already been vacated? They're expected to run the department or business as if they've been working in the company for the past three years! Be sure to instruct the new hire on their responsibilities and tasks, enabling them to take on the position quickly.

Outsourcing

When your car needs to be repaired, do you spend hours trying to fix it or see a mechanic who takes two hours? Do you do your own tax return or have an accountant prepare it for you? If you need a new assistant, do you place an ad in the paper, spend hours interviewing people, or have a recruitment company do all the groundwork and send you the top three applicants?

Why waste your precious time on tasks that will do exactly that…waste your precious time. Time is money!

Use the Experts

Use the valuable input of experts who can take away the stress and hassle and carry out the tasks in a fraction of the time it would take you. Sure, you have to pay for it, but isn't it better to work smarter, not harder?

Why spend hours on tasks that are not your specialty?

Identify what you do best and then delegate or outsource the rest. In fact, if you truly feel you are good at what you do and are happy to share that, why not teach someone else those same skills, then you could really leverage yourself.

If you are a business owner, this will allow you more time to work on your business rather than in it.

A Word of Caution for Business Owners

Be careful about who you get your advice from. I know of many small business owners who listen to the advice of their personal assistants, spouses, and relatives on how to run their businesses, although those people have never been in business themselves.

By all means, get feedback from your people; however, if you really want to work smarter, not harder, then invest some money into a business coach or someone who has already run a successful business so that you can avoid costly mistakes and have someone else offer a fresh perspective. Being too closely involved can give you a tainted view.

Write down all your responsibilities and the tasks that you undertake. Tick the tasks that someone else could realistically do. Then, write next to each one either the name of the person or type of person/company who can do this for you or offer some expert assistance or support, e.g., bookkeeper, printing company, personal assistant, coach.

To work smarter not harder, always look at who else can do this work/task. Always look at lightening your load so that you can spend your time doing what you do best.

Many online business owners struggle with working too hard for not enough return. Even when the returns are good, the hours can be gruelling. As a father and husband,

I can't afford to be sitting at my computer 24/7. I chose to run an online business because I want to be home with my kids, but at home glued to a computer screen isn't like being at home.

Even if you don't have a kid or a spouse, a business should not become your entire life.

It's a recipe for burnout and a dismal life that revolves around a computer. At first, building your business and working may seem exciting, but then you look up and realize there's nothing else in your life.

So, how do you work smarter and not harder? In other words, how do you make more money with less personal time invested in your business?

To me, it comes down to four key points:

1. Value Your Time:

You need to set and limit your working hours. You probably run your business so you can stay home with your family and have more freedom. Well, being a prisoner to your computer doesn't do either of those things for you.

When you limit your work time, you are more productive. If you have only three hours to get work done, you are more likely to stay focused and do what you need to do. If you have set aside the whole day to work, you'll probably slack off and hang out at forums, check your stats endlessly, or find other distractions.

2. Leverage the Strength & Time of Others:

Don't think of yourself as a solo entrepreneur...think of yourself as a team. You can leverage the strength and time of others by:

- Outsourcing: Never try to do it all yourself!
- Partnering with others reaching the same target market as you: Your competition doesn't need to be your enemy. Make them your partners instead!
- Recruiting and training an affiliate force: Just setting up the script for your affiliate program isn't enough...set up a stellar program instead.
- Being part of a mastermind group: Share business strategies and experiences.

"You may find someone in the group that is a perfect fit to work on a project with you."

Stephanie Burns

3. Implement Passive Income Models into Your Business:

Outsourcing and having your own well-managed affiliate program are ways to generate passive income. Other ways to add more passive income to your online business are:

- Join affiliate programs: You don't have to fulfill all the orders and provide customer support yourself.

- Learn **search engine optimization (SEO)**: Search engine optimization is an excellent source of highly targeted traffic for your website. Just think, people enter a keyword phrase for something they want and voila, they find you.

- Implement pay-per-click strategies: Just like with search engines, you can get high-targeted traffic to your website, but you have to pay for it. But setting up a cost-effective and profitable campaign can do wonders for your business. Try AdWords of Yahoo Search Marketing.

- Use **autoresponders**: Effectively automate your follow-up process with your prospects and customers.

- Backend sales & upsells: When someone is already going to buy from you once, they are likely to buy more. Make sure you make extra offers.

4. Embrace Technology:

This one might be tough for some non-technical people. Honestly, I'm not very technical and I get intimidated by technology...but I do know that if I can automate something in my business, it saves me time and money. That's why I have a programmer on hand to help me with stuff like this. I don't have to implement the technology myself. I just use it to my advantage in my business.

Some uses of technology can include:

- Autoresponders
- Shopping carts
- Membership sites
- Automating content addition to your sites
- Making customer/prospect management easier and more profitable
- Customer feedback, comments, reviews
- Affiliate program
- Tracking advertising and split testing

Please, prioritize your work! Your business, family, and friends will thank you for it!

Lie Down on the Ground & Realise No Job is Beneath You

If you do not have any money behind your venture or have very little, then you need to be able to support yourself while you are building your empire. This means having an income. Do not be so arrogant as to think that your business is going to bathe you in money from day one. For most, it takes time and effort, but it will occur once all the stars align.

Having an income while you build your business is important as it gives you the revenue you need to complete the things you need money for. It also reduces the stress on you to bring home the bacon and your other half (if you have one) will look at you with fondness and love instead of dread and terror.

I have done all sorts of jobs over my lifetime and some of them I didn't like, but I stuck them out simply because we needed the money to survive. It was not always a perfect situation but at least it was money coming in.

Andrew was a friend of mine, and many years ago, he was a highly qualified and successful accountant. He wanted to start a new venture in the photography field (he loved taking photos of cars; he had tens of thousands of photographs of them) but did not really have much of an idea as to what he wanted to do. But he mentioned that he did have about $12,500 in the bank to get it going. After some initial discussion and comments back and forth, I suggested to him that he build a website and offer the photographs up for free to the public to use. Yes, I know he could have sold them, but this was back in the day when CPM and PPC were just starting out, and there was real money to be made through it if done right. I could see the potential if the marketing and promotion were good enough. We spoke about it for a while longer, and I suggested to him he would need to do whatever it takes to achieve his goal and to always focus on the objective.

That was on a Thursday night. The following Tuesday, I got a phone call from him saying he had some news he wanted to share. I drove over to his house and we sat down to chat. He laid out on the table his plan and what he wanted to do. He had been busy, but I also could sense this was not what he wanted to tell me. And then he shared what he had meant to.

He said he had had a moment of clarity over the weekend and a vision of what his site would become. He had gone to work on the money and given notice so that he could spend 100% of his time on his own business.

Well, I was stunned, shocked, dismayed, bewildered, and all those other words of disbelief. What he had done was, in effect, cut off the only source of income he had.

When I say you will need to step up and do whatever it takes to achieve your goals, that includes doing the jobs you don't want to do. It does *not* mean giving up a source of income, and it certainly does not mean giving up the *only* source of income you have.

Once the realization of what he had done set in he decided to get another job and quickly so that at least he had some money coming in. He looked for a job for about three weeks and then, one day, said he was sick of applying. I then suggested to him to apply for something not in his field. He laughed, and I didn't think he would give it another thought. One week later, he called me and said he got a part-time job as a cleaner for a shopping centre. Not the same sort of money he was making as an accountant, but an income nonetheless. From that point on, he devoted his life to getting his business going.

About four years later, he sold the site to another company for a tidy sum and retired. At the time he sold it, he had over 123,400 photographs online and was making about $85,000 a year just from advertising revenue from the site. Sadly, my friend passed away of cancer in 2017, but I will never forget his commitment to doing whatever it took to get the job done.

The emotional beast of Buying Low & Selling High

When it comes to investing, there is a method to make money where you buy shares when the price is low and sell them when the price is high. It's pretty standard, and for many, it is a staple of their operations.

In business, there is also a similar philosophy that can be described as somewhat of an opposite position. Acting on strategies when the chips are down is not a safe place to be. The margins for safety are much lower in the short term. To be successful, you need to act on your strategies when you are having a good streak and things are moving. In plain terms, act when the iron is hot.

Business is an emotional beast. It has a mind of its own and a heartbeat to match. This is why you need to be focused on the strategies and not let your emotions control your decision-making. Sure, you feel ecstatic when things are going well, but just as emotionally charged is when things are not going well. This is when we again tend to make rash decisions and desperate plays to try and recoup position or share. During this sort of situation, we tend to make decisions that we would normally never do when we are focused, relaxed, and thinking straight.

Taking small wins consistently all the time adds up to big wins over time. When we are rising, we should be looking for the wins we know we can get and develop marketing plans and strategies that will help secure your footing. If wins are predictable, then this may be a good thing. Less risk means less loss.

Sometimes, and hopefully not often, there are situations where you should not action an issue to save a sale. Sometimes, it is best to let the loss ride out and recoup. It might be less expensive to let the loss happen than it would be to try and recover the loss. I have seen it happen in business, where people chase the loss, trying to rebuild a relationship, redevelop a new product, or rework an idea. For these people, time is all it will take till they lose everything.

Focusing on what you can control and what you cannot makes all the difference. Buying low and selling high is a great position to be in if the signs tell you to, but acting on these same two ideas is business-shattering if the signs say one thing, but you think your gut is saying something different. This is where confusion, doubt, and questioning come into play, and they can play hard, causing you to lose sight of the end goal.

Procrastinators get confused with this train of thought all the time. They focus on a section of the business so hard and for so long that when the time comes to action something relevant to the section they have been working on, it becomes apparent that the time for that idea has passed. There was no action (no sell) to make a successful play on the action. Or the complete opposite or some combination of it can also be true. This is why a clear focus on the goal is paramount all the time. Then, small victories along the way will become obvious, and actions happen more often. Even though they may not be complete, they still scratch up wins for you consistently.

I'm not an expert in this field by a long shot, and there are many more experienced people than me out there, but the one thing I have learnt over my life is that if you lose sight of the objective, the end goal makes no difference in what you do because you are just moving forwards to nowhere.

Keep your eye on the goal. Stay focused, win the fights you can, and walk away from the fights you can't. Wasting time on something you cannot win or takes too long to win is unproductive and will cost you more than it may have been worth.

Some people may think that you can do too much, especially when marketing is concerned, but my experience in this is far different. Your wins come from people knowing about you and your products. Do not make the mistake of thinking your customers will feel overpromoted or spammed. They are not all seeing everything you are doing. Social media does not work like a funnel for all ads going to the same person every time. It is a selective process that algorithms spit out.

Gary Vaynerchuk recently said, "When I'm putting out 64 pieces of content a day for a brand, my hope is that the customer I'm targeting may see that piece of content one day a week. And the 64 pieces are actually going to 30 different groups. So it's only two pieces of content a day, and that too viewed on a [mobile] screen." This is a simple and very straightforward way to look at all your marketing capacity.

Unleash your NINJA and be ready to Pivot

I like to watch some sports but would not call myself a sporty person. I think I watch because I like to think that people may see me as a more sporty-minded person. I'm not, but I do learn a few things by watching different sports. Netball is one I find very interesting because the speed at which the game is played is amazing, yet every player is stopping their feet constantly so as to not travel. They move on their feet from one side to the other, allowing them to make a play and pass the ball or shoot for the net. This is called pivoting.

As a business owner, you have to be prepared to do the same, especially when an opportunity presents itself that allows you to move forward toward your goal, even when it does not quite fall into the plan you had laid out at the start.

"Engage people with what they expect; it is what they are able to discern and confirms their projections. It settles them into predictable patterns of response, occupying their minds while you wait for the extraordinary moment — that which they cannot anticipate."

Sun Tzu

Pivots come in all shapes and sizes, but they all do the same thing. They make you shift from one point of reference or action to another. The complexity comes when you try to understand the benefit of the pivot in the business model.

Let me explain.

Say you are going to create a business as a shoemaker, and you want to create a range of new shoes made from the finest leather you can buy. You have the skills and equipment and the money, but you suddenly realise that the leather is not possible to get in the quantities you need. What do you do? Some would say hold out till it becomes available. Good idea, though that could spill out to weeks or months possibly even years. This decision has made you exactly nothing while you wait.

Now let's consider the same situation, but this time, you decided to use a slightly different leather and produce a medium-level entry shoe. The quality is the same, the design is the same, yet the price is more suited to the general market of shoe wearers. Now, instead of not making money, you potentially are making good money and creating a customer base. This base should become your **feeder** to the potential new top-line range. This is where your pivot reaps rewards. See, all those people who are buying your shoes now become an instant market for your top-shelf range. Less marketing is required because they know your quality. There is less cost because there is less marketing. Simple.

Many people would choose to wait instead. I have found that this causes a loss of confidence, a lack of desire, and a drop in productivity. These are all the signs of a potential procrastinator. If you want to make shoes, THEN MAKE SHOES.

Here are 10 examples from Jason Nazar of Forbes.com on some truly great Pivots in the business world.

Twitter

The most legendary pivot in social media history is the transformation of Odeo into Twitter. Odeo began as a network where people could find and subscribe to podcasts, but the founders feared the company's demise when iTunes began taking over the podcast niche. After giving the employees two weeks to come up with new ideas, the company decided to make a drastic change and run with the idea of a status-updating micro-blogging platform conceived by Jack Dorsey and Biz Stone.

PayPal

PayPal has always focused on payments, but it has gone through many permutations. It was developed by a company called Confinity in 1999 to allow people to "beam" payments from their PDAs (handheld digital computers, such as the Palm Pilot, an early incarnation of the smartphone). After merging with a financial services company called X.com, PayPal became the preferred online payment system for eBay sellers, which propelled its name into payment processing fame.

Groupon

In 2007, Andrew Mason created a website called The Point, which was a "social good" fundraising site that ran on a "tipping point" system, where a cause would only receive funding once the pledged donations reached a certain number. Mason started Groupon as a side project, which applied a similar "tipping point" concept to local deals: if enough people pledged to do an activity, they would unlock a discount on it. The Groupon project quickly eclipsed The Point in popularity and became the daily deal tycoon we know today.

Starbucks

The coffee shop, which now inhabits every street corner (and sometimes two on each street corner), did not always sell fresh-brewed coffee to customers. They started off in 1971 selling espresso makers and coffee beans, which Howard Schultz (current chairman, president and CEO) fell in love with on first taste. After his visit to Italy in 1983, Schultz was determined to actually brew and sell Starbucks coffee in a European-style coffeehouse and transformed Starbucks into the nationwide java sensation it has become today.

Flickr

Flickr actually began as an online role-playing game called Game Neverending, where users would travel around a digital map, interact with other users, and buy, sell, and build items. The game also included a photo-sharing tool, which turned out to be one of the most popular aspects of the game. The company decided to leverage this photo popularity and pivot to Flickr, which was acquired by Yahoo! in 2005 and became one of its most beloved and successful acquisitions.

HP

Hewlett-Packard has shifted focus since it launched as an engineering company in 1947. It began by creating a slew of electrical testing products, including audio and signal generators, but in 1968 introduced the first large-scale personal computer. Personal consumer-friendly computers did not catch on until the 1990s when HP focused solely on getting Americans to buy home computers and diverged the production of their testing equipment into a separate company. Since then, it has focused mainly on computers and printing/scanning accessories.

Instagram

Instagram is the most widely used photo app for iPhone, but many don't know its origins. Instagram began as Burbn, a check-in app that included gaming elements from Mafia Wars and a photo element as well. The creators worried Burbn had too much clutter and potential actions and would never gain traction. So they took a risk and stripped all the features but one: photos. They rebuilt a version of the app that focused solely on photography—it was clean and simple, and clearly, it paid off.

Wrigley

Wrigley didn't always sell gum. In fact, William Wrigley Jr. stumbled on the value of gum while giving it away for free. Mr. Wrigley Jr. moved to Chicago in the 1890s and took up work as a soap and baking powder salesman. He got the idea of offering free chewing gum with his purchases, and the gum proved to be more popular than his actual product. Wrigley went on to manufacture his own chewing gum brands, Juicy Fruit, Spearmint, and eventually Doublemint. Today the company grosses billions in revenue and is one of the most recognizable brands in American history.

Pinterest

This incredibly popular "pinning" social network pivoted from "Tote," which allowed people to browse and shop their favourite retailers and sent them updates when their favourite items were available and on sale. The creators realized that the users of Tote were mostly interested in building "collections" of their favourite items and sharing these collections with friends. Since its repositioning, Pinterest now has over 70 million users, with approximately 80% of its users being women. While its pivot has been wildly successful in terms of user growth,

Pinterest is trying to figure out how to get back to Tote's e-commerce and revenue roots.

Suzuki

This automotive company may be best known in the U.S. for their high-performance motorcycles and sports vehicles. But from 1910 to 1935 Michio Suzuki was best known as the inventor and purveyor of weaving loom machines that powered Japan's silk industry. An inventor at heart, Suzuki started looking for other products to produce in the interest of diversification. Suzuki's complete 180 might have even given the founders of Odeo and Twitter pause. In either case, it's all quite tweet-worthy.

Less is More (Except with Jelly Beans)

I remember the day my dad brought home the first computer I ever saw in real life. It was an amazing piece of technology and was something that forever changed the way I looked at information. I would watch him work on it, writing documents, only to then see them printed out on a printer that sounded like a saw cutting through plastic. It was an amazing machine and I always wanted to sit in front of it and have a go.

Over time, technology got better and better, yet he never really upgraded the computer. Sure, he did some minor things but nothing of substance. I always wondered why he didn't, and as far as I could see, there was nothing that told me the answer.

Then, one year, about 22 years after I had left home, I was speaking to him, and I happened to ask him that very question: "Why did you never upgrade the computer?"

His answer was plain and simple and has stuck with me. He said that the computer did what he needed it to do. No new upgrade would do anything different than what he needed it to. He said that keeping it simple meant he could focus on other things. He felt that sometimes less was more.

I often lay awake wondering how I could gain more while doing less. Then, one day, I came across a term that would forever change my life (well, I wanted it to). Passive Income, it's called, and I obsess over it sometimes. But like always, I bring myself back to reality quickly when I realize that effort requires work, and nothing can be gained on a free ride.

Many business owners or people wanting to start a business often fall into the trap of thinking that quantity of effort results in greater success instead of understanding that *quality* of effort can have just the same if not more of an impact… if handled right.

This misconception of having to do more to be more successful is just plain wrong and a bad way to look at business. There are people out there that we have put up on pedestals as experts and leaders in their fields, and I have even heard some say that if you want to succeed in life, then you must work 20 hours a day. Work as hard as you can as long as you can and you might make it. Frankly, this is absurd advice and shocking to think that it is given.

I am not saying that hard work is not required — on the contrary! What I am saying is that strategically working is far more effective and far less dangerous to your health and sanity.

I have heard the phrase "Business Minimalism" floating around over the last few years, and I like it. It sounds interesting when you say it in the same sentence with other words like "Focus" or "Quality".

I developed a theory many years ago and taught it many times in workshops for university and to small businesses. It was called "The Cornflake Theory".

The theory stated that the simple things in life were often the best. Yes, just like the advert said, growing up for those of us old enough to remember.

In essence it was that a bowl of cornflakes is a great start to any day. Each flake of corn was created from a single kernel, transformed into flat crispy disks of delight that can fill a bowl and make a morning seem delightful, yet even a single flake for me and I have since found out, for many others, gives just as much pleasure and joy.

In 1878, when John Harvey Kellogg was inventing cornflakes with his brother Will Keith Kellogg, they did not mean to create small circular disks from the start. No, in fact, the story is that they were trying to create a much larger sheet of dough. The flake was a simple accident, but it turned out to be the greatest cereal ever invented (well, in my opinion). This simple and inexpensive accident led to many delights in food we have today. However, this single disk of flattened corn became their Minimal Viable Product (more on that later) that the brothers needed to go on to build an empire.

Using that same theory of keeping things simple, we as business owners should be trying to stick with our strengths and focus on the small things and get them right. We should work on large-scale plans by breaking them down into smaller, more manageable tasks. Collectively, these tasks, these flakes of business, add up to one big successful outcome: the proverbial bowl of cornflakes that you can sit down and enjoy. Creating passive streams of income that do not rely on huge efforts continually can be just as rewarding as a good bowl of cornflakes.

Gayle Sato wrote a great article in 2020 on what passive income was. She said earning passive income can be a great way to supplement your income, whether you use it to make a few extra dollars here and there or invest significant time and money to build a major income stream. Although just about anyone might welcome a little extra money, for independent contractors with sporadic income, stay-at-home parents, full-time students, and retirees, passive income can be especially valuable.

Gale also mentioned cultivating passive income takes some active research and, often, more than a little work. But the payoff can be significant. Having a stream of income that's not dependent on employment or contracting can be a hedge against lean economic times or help enrich your retirement. Whether you generate a little passive income or a lot, the security of having more than one source of money is in itself a reward.

I know it's strange and maybe even a little weird, but I can assure you that if a single kernel (one small business) created the perfect way to give joy, just imagine what a whole bowl of them (streams of passive come) would do for you.

Pack a Tent, Time to go Hunting for Opportunities

In this modern technology-driven world, one cannot help but wonder what tomorrow will bring. So much change in industry, markets, communities, and countries leads to the realization that new ideas must be springing up all the time.

One of the core skills you need when developing a business or looking to expand a business is what to look for. The opportunities that are out there that can help you achieve your goals. Not only that, you also need to know how to use them and take advantage of them when you find them.

Let's not forget that waiting for the opportunities to come to you may be a long waiting game, so you need to go out and find them. Seek out those rare and elusive sparks of creativity that can be honed and polished into something grand, and when you find them, you need to know how to keep them close and ward off any potential rivals that want to take it away from you.

So, I suppose you're thinking: how do I do it? Or what do I need to know on how to do it? Good questions. Let's run through a few of the more pressing ones to learn.

Speed. That's right, speed. A marathon runner does not use their main power and energy at the start of a race. They manage their pace and focus their attention on maintaining a steady and disciplined approach. Only when the time is right do they turn the speed on and use the reserve power they have had ready for that moment. They wait till the field is set for them to take advantage and then they go. Now, more often than not, the person who does this first will streak out ahead. This is where they then try to stay by using all the tools and skills they have been taught and trained to use. See, speed must be used correctly.

As a businessperson, you need to know when to run and when to walk. This comes from doing your homework on opportunities and assessing their effect on the market.

Consistency. This is more for those who cannot keep track and manage time well. Procrastinators, listen up. Once you start on a road to growth and begin looking for opportunities, you cannot stop until you have the one(s) you want. You need to persist in the drive that first led you to look. It takes effort to keep going, especially after you meet the proverbial brick wall time and time again. But if you can, then you will achieve the prize and win the race.

Strength. Being brave is not always about standing up to a bully or jumping off a bridge. Sometimes, it is conquering your own fears and sticking to your guns when things begin to struggle and problems arise. You need to stand tall and back the decisions you make based on good research. You need to be competent enough to know when to zig and when to zag so as to evade the traps along the way.

"You cannot be anything you want to be—but you can be a lot more of who you already are."

Tom Rath

Nourishment. Once you have the opportunity and can see it blending into your established pipeline, you need to stay with it. So many business owners fall short of the mark on this—it's astounding.

A decade after webpages became an advertising channel, companies wanted to be online. They wanted a digital presence. This became a must, and I saw and spoke to literally dozens of firms who wanted their own website. I would ask them why, to which almost all of them said, "We want a digital presence so we can be seen around the world."

A noble idea, I thought, but one that lacked any real substance other than keeping up with the Joneses. There was a fundamental flaw in their thinking which so many off them failed to even see until it was pointed out to them. They had forgotten that marketing also was required, not to mention site maintenance and upkeep.

One company I was consulting for desperately wanted a website. They asked me to help find them a programmer so they could get it done before Christmas. It was a simple gig and not complicated, considering it was October. Finding a programmer was not too difficult as it was the new thing, and I was working at a university surrounded by kids learning this stuff. The site was built in 4 weeks, ready for December to roll around. It was a great opportunity they were doing, and if done right, they would be a winner for sure. I finished up my tasks and left them excited and eager to bath in their future earnings.

The site was good as far as sites were concerned. Good graphics, strong content, great images, and some impressive deals and specials. They had even spent some money on securing a high-profile basketball player to be a model for them on their front page. The thing was, though, that in early January, I heard from them asking for some help.

During their so called "Impact Period" for sales, they had expected to raise in excess of $125,000 from the site. They had planned and calculated and had come up with what they thought was a conservative figure. They made less than a fifth of that. The actual site had cost them more than what they had made.

When I had them all in the room, I said with a frankness to my voice, "What marketing have you done to let people know about the site?" You guessed it…none.

It is like building an amazing store with the greatest products, services, and deals in the world. You're bound to make money when people come in, but if you do not tell them where you are, then how in all things holy do you expect to make money from it? Don't waste the opportunity once you have it. Maximize it until it returns the favour.

If You Can't Stand the Heat, Stop Running into the Fire

Like all excited business creators, there will come a time when you find yourself at a point of making a serious decision that will determine which way your business will go. And yes, in some circumstances, that decision means up or down, too.

The statement "If you can't stand the heat, get out of the kitchen" by Harry S Truman is a comment on the ethics or principle of a position or problem. Poker players are often heard stating this as ethical dilemmas amongst friends are often part of the poker mentality, though a player will happily bluff their way through a hand to take the rewards away from their friends. Taking the last of your friend's chips on a bluff and watching them get frustrated as they see what they lost against is a classic time to boast and brag about the kitchen and its heat.

However, I look at it in a slightly different aspect. Not so much as one coming from an ethical perspective or moral judgment, but rather that of good sense and common understanding of your own limitations.

Just recently, I was asked to help project manage a redevelopment of a website for online learning. It was an interesting project and the person I was helping I have known for a while. I had done projects like this before and was a little apprehensive about it, but I took it on as I liked the idea this company stood for and what they were trying to do. I had not worked with the person before, so I was not coming into it with any preconceived notions.

Things went well at first, and an outline of what was needed was discussed. I told them that the price they had been given was way too high for what they were wanting and that it should not take three months as indicated to them from other people. I put together a programmer I had heard of and we agreed on a price. Looking back, it was probably a little light but that's the risk.

Programming commenced, and everything seemed to be going well. I had mentioned to the person that this was not going to be a fast process at first as there was a lot of coding to do, so they should not expect big movements in the first few weeks. However, at the end of the very first week, when we had a video meeting with the programmer and the client, I noticed something I had not noticed earlier. Concern on the part of the client was already evident. The questions they were asking were already the exact issues I had spoken of with them about time and processes and that things could not be rushed.

The second week's meeting went the same with even more concern being expressed through several emails and phone calls. I again reinforced the same points about process and functionality and that this takes most of the time, so patience was required. Sadly, as it continued, the calls became less positive and more issue-focused. The exact thing I had said would happen was happening. I had made it very clear that letting clients see a project too soon would result in the problems that were arising and now I was in the thick of it.

I wrote several emails explaining things, but it did little to change the client's perspective, who I could now tell was frustrated and questioning the entire venture. The entire project was now consuming my time as I worried about having to speak to the client again, knowing that I would only be asked the same questions again. I was staying up at night thinking about it and trying to figure out why this person did not understand what we were telling them.

So, I had to make a decision.

The third-week meeting was postponed due to personal issues with the programmer for several days, but I decided to write an email to the client and explain that due to the issues surrounding the concerns and frustration, I said that all communication should now go directly to the programmer and that I was bowing out of the project. I was not being paid for any of my time anyway, so I was not concerned about bailing. However, I did say I would pay the last milestone payment for the project and finish with the programmer the requirements of the quote so the client was no longer in any more financial risk of the quote we had agreed on. I wanted to leave the project with a clear conscience. Yes, it would cost me money, and yes, I did feel a bit sad about the process. However, I felt a weight lifted off my shoulders when I sent the email.

I'm not one to complain or to cry over things like this, but it does show that sometimes you need to bail on a project if the situation is becoming so toxic that it is disrupting everything else. Decisions like this can come in all sorts of disguises and sometimes you do not see them approaching, but when you do, you may have to make a decision that will cost you money in the short term but save your sanity and focus in the long term.

Considering dropping a project, product, or service in order to move forward with your objectives and goals is a part of good decision-making. Don't make these decisions out of laziness or ill will. Make them from a position of purpose and conscious decision as to whether it is improving your focus or reducing it, whether it is costing you money or making you money.

Fighting May Be Needed, but Combat Is Optional

There are times when you should stand up and be ready to fight for what you believe in and sometimes these fights will be hard to handle, which is why you need to pick them carefully. Fighting should always be a last resort and it is most definitely always optional.

When I read the phrase by well-known US author Max Lucado, "Conflict is inevitable, combat is optional," I thought about the types of conflicts you may have as a business owner. I have also had some good ones. Some were good, some hard, and some downright funny, but all of them were situations I found myself in because I had, for the most part, not prepared myself sufficiently to handle the oncoming conflict.

There will always be conflict in business. You will not always agree with your production staff over how something must be put together, or you may disagree with a client over how a website should be designed, or maybe you may even have it out with your significant other about the amount of money you need to spend on a project, but that does not mean that things have to escalate to a combat situation.

I was in the Army Reserves for a time and loved it. I think had I not injured my back, I would have proceeded to make a career out of it. Needless to say, combat was what we were training for, and I was truly good at what I did. However, one aspect of my personal life did not sit well with some. I did not drink or smoke as it was against my religion. As a member of the Church of Jesus Christ of Latter-day Saints, I live by a health code, and so I have never drunk or smoked. I owe most of that success to my big brother, who would have beaten me had I ever tried it anyway. I always looked up to him even though he did those things, and to this day, I thank him for keeping me away from those types of products.

I once had a situation where I was required to go to a special dinner on base. It was a dinner for some dignitaries, and I was asked to attend. It was an honour, and I gladly accepted. I went home and told my wife and friends about this awesome opportunity.

I was given a document explaining the protocol on the night, and to my complete horror, there was a special toast that was to be carried out, and a traditional decanter of sherry would be used for all in attendance to toast with.

This would have been an issue, without a doubt. So, I tried to arrange to meet my Commanding Officer and for the most bizarre reasons, I was never able to get hold of him before dinner. Even on the night, I could not get two seconds with the man. I found myself at the table, surrounded by years of experience and tradition: Sergeants, Captains, Colonels, Majors, and a Lieutenant General. I was truly at the wrong table.

The time came, and the waiters all poured the glasses. I did not stop them from pouring mine, though I'm not sure why, and when we were asked to stand, I stood, taking the glass in my hand. The toast was given, and I raised my glass but did not drink. I immediately looked at my CO and caught the stare I was waiting for. It resembled a needle entering my eyes and exiting out the bottom of my back. I was done for, I knew it. I was half expecting his to explode right there in front of everyone. This was not a man to mince words.

After the dinner was over and constantly trying to stay out of arm's length, it happened. The hand on the shoulder and the forced turning of my body. Face to face with my destiny, I waited for the inevitable dressing down I was about to receive.

To my surprise, he said that he had considered my beliefs when he had invited me and knew that he was putting me in a situation I was not going to be comfortable with. He had purposefully been sidestepping me as he wanted to see what I would do. See, he knew my principles and convictions and hoped that I would stay true to them, no matter what, and was delighted that I did. He told to me that he had great admiration for a person who would stand by his convictions in the face of adversity and wanted to thank me for not betraying them.

From that day onwards, and nearly 38 years later, I have never betrayed my convictions for anything. I hold my integrity as my highest strength and am grateful for what I learned. I did not have to fight the system to win the battle. I only had to stand my ground and know I was making the best choice. Conflict and combat did not have to enter the story for me to come out, in my eyes, a winner.

Many years later, at a business dinner in Shenzhen, China, a similar thing happened with a table full of very wealthy men. The Chinese love their alcohol, and I stood my ground when they asked me consistently about joining in. It took a few rounds and some discussions as to why I did not drink, and for the most part, I did not know what they were speaking about, but to this day, I count one of those men as one of my closest friends because he stood up for me in that situation. We still work together on projects and have a strong friendship of respect and trust. Thanks, Sunly.

Don't Confuse Efforts with Results

Read the title again, carefully. It doesn't mean "It takes more effort to get results." It means "It takes more *than* effort to get results." Ah, the difference a word can make.

In the world that I grew up and live in, hard work is considered a high virtue. I've read children's books that spoke of the value of hard work. I grew up on a farm and was proud to work hard. Few compliments will be viewed as highly as, "they are a hard worker." And most people I know consider persistence a highly valued trait.

And I suspect your world is much the same.

As I continue to learn and observe the world around me, I'm quite sure this isn't the whole story.

That doesn't mean I don't think effort is required, that work is necessary, or that action helps us reach our goals. Of course, we need to take action to get results. Work is required to achieve anything of value. The quarrel I have is not with the word "work." It's with the word "hard."

Some things are hard work and always will be. However, hard work, taken to the extreme, leads us to the equivalent of bashing our heads against a concrete wall, figuring that eventually, the wall will crack, and we will break through. Can we break through the concrete wall and reach our objective using our heads? Perhaps, but I believe there are better ways to break through the wall!

"I've got a theory that if you give 100 percent all of the time, somehow things will work out in the end."

Larry Bird

While this analogy may be simple and somewhat painful, I believe it holds an important element of truth for us all. Why? We all know there are better ways to break through a concrete wall than using our heads. As you read this, I'm sure you can think of many tools that would allow you to use them more easily and successfully while creating less pain and agony for yourself.

Unfortunately, people often feel that hard work is necessary, and that sacrifice is required for them to reach the things they desire.

The truth is that what we really need to do is work intelligently. There are many things we can do to work more intelligently, including building our skills, our capacities, our network, and our experience. All of these things are important. But none of them are the most important.

What is the Most Important?

The most important key to reaching our objectives, with less "hard" work, is within ourselves. The most

215

important keys are the natural gifts and talents that lie within us, largely untapped and unrecognized.

In my experience there are two ways to mop the floor: on your hands and knees using a rag or standing up using a mop. When we celebrate hard work, it's like we are celebrating the rag. If all you have is a rag, you can certainly get the floor clean. On the other hand, if you knew there was a mop, would you choose the rag?

So, it is with our own natural gifts. We have the mop, but we don't often think about it or recognize it and, therefore, don't use it.

A close friend and sounding board of mine, Peter O'Callaghan has always been someone I could bounce ideas off and get an honest opinion about projects I have wanted to do. I do not always get the answers I want, but I am willing to listen. I have, at times, taken his advice, and it has worked, and then other times, it has not, and it has cost me greatly.

Peter has often said to me, "You are too nice. You do too much for other people and forget about yourself. Stop giving everything away all the time." You what? When I look back on the things I have done, he is right. I put off so many opportunities for myself to help others that it became a bit of a detriment. I'm not saying it's a bad thing, but I am saying there needs to be balance in all things.

Here are three things you can do today to begin to work more intelligently:

Identify your gifts and strengths. In order to use the mop, you must know the mop exists. In order for us to take advantage of our unique talents, abilities, strengths, and gifts, we must know they are there. This requires us to think about our strengths and ask others what our strengths are. It will require time for reflection. It will require time. This task itself will require some effort. But the effort is worth it. Every time we use the mop, we gain time, save energy, and complete a task more rapidly. It's time to find your mop!

Do not think you have to be everything to everyone. Sometimes, you will have projects in front of you that look good and are of real interest to you. This is when you have to decide if helping this project become a success will lead you towards your own success. This is tough, especially when helping others may be your nature. You have to know when to say no and focus on the main objective.

Allow yourself to use them. Once we know we have a mop, we must allow ourselves to use it. Maybe your mentor used a rag. Maybe your mother used a rag. While that might be the most successful way for them, that doesn't necessarily mean it is for you. Once you identified your gifts and talents, you must allow yourself to use them. You must take the opportunity to use your unique gifts, because in using them, your results will seemingly flow from you.

Work on building them. Many of us, when reviewing our skills, will identify a list of both strengths and weaknesses. This is an excellent exercise. While it is important for us to recognize our weaknesses and work in many cases to improve them, it is equally important to continue to nurture and strengthen our greatest gifts and strengths. Consider spending at least as much time nurturing and building your strengths as you do on improving or fixing your areas of weakness. Again, you will get greater results for these efforts because they will come easier and more naturally.

When you do these three things, you'll begin to make your work easier and more enjoyable. At the same time, you will most likely find that your results will come sooner and more completely.

What could be better than that? The results we want, with less effort and more enjoyment. Remember, it takes more than effort to get results; it takes intelligent, informed, enlightened, effort.

It's time to get to work.

Using Your Internet Efforts to Produce Results

The internet today comes with promises of wealth and fame. This allows many to dream of riches and notoriety. The opportunity is out there, but the fact is that most people don't have a clue how to get there.

So many think that they can achieve prosperity by just showing up. Unfortunately, that is not the way this ball bounces.

Is there a simple answer? I don't think there is a single simple answer, yet how to be successful on the internet is pretty basic: you have to be willing to work. But work at what, you may ask?

The first thing is to work hard at learning everything you can about your chosen field. I suggest reading and studying the people who have had success in the past. There is an endless supply of knowledge floating around out there, and you want to read as much of it as you can.

When I first started trying to make a living on the net, I thought I was wise enough to do it on my own. It sure didn't take long to figure out that it was a joke. When I started paying attention to what some of the successful marketers were doing, I started making money myself.

People pay thousands of dollars to go to college to get the information needed to be successful, yet most are not willing to pay a hundred dollars for educational information on the Internet. This is not to say that you should spend thousands of dollars on an internet education, but there is information worth paying for.

Now that you have read a bit and read some more, you are ready to start working on the Internet. It is now time to put in some more of that hard work. Work is the key ingredient to getting you where you want to go.

Part of the learning experience is to learn *how* to work. When I first started on the net, I wasted a lot of valuable time. The problem was that I didn't know what kind of work was worth the time. This is part of the education that comes with experience. You will find that managing your time well is very important. It may be time to read some more.

The internet is a great place for anyone who wants to work — and work is the key word. There is money to be made, but it is not going to jump in your lap just because you showed up.

Here are some interesting websites I use that you may find helpful:

Fiver: https://www.fiverr.com/ Find people who can help you do just about anything. I actually spend time on this just looking for things to help me or give me support, and boy, does it pay off. I used Fiver to help edit and lay out this book as well as the design of the cover.

Upwork: https://www.upwork.com/ If you want a website, phone app, or software written, this is the place. Great value and excellent service. I have several programmers I use all the time now because they are so good. Has saved me thousands.

Codepen: https://codepen.io/ CodePen is a social development environment for front-end designers and developers. Build and deploy a website, show off your work, build test cases to learn and debug, and find inspiration right on your screen live. It can get a bit addictive.

Pixabay: https://pixabay.com/ Almost 2 million totally free images, videos, vector artwork, and graphics. It's a site I still use a lot, and I often go and find images for projects for all sorts of things.

Morguefiles: https://morguefile.com/ Another site like Pixabay but different, Michael, Kevin, Johannes and Emily have really made a great site for free images.

Thingiverse: https://www.thingiverse.com/ Need a 3D File for a metric screw measuring device or a sanding tool adaptor. Maybe you love cosplay and need a Mandalorian Helmet. This is the place to find the files you need for 3D Printing. You can spend hours here looking through all the cool stuff.

Envato Market: https://themeforest.net/ offers almost 50,000 WordPress Themes and website Templates starting from $2. If one site has saved me money when it comes to ideas, it's this one. I love the variety of scripts available.

Speechnotes: https://speechnotes.co/ Can't be bothered typing then sit back and let this little puppy do the typing. Simply click on the mic and start talking. This beauty transcribes for you in real time.

PDFEscape:

https://www.pdfescape.com/?noredirect=true If you can not afford professional PDF creator software, then then this is the one for you. You can edit and create PDF documents online or download the desktop version and do it right from your computer.

Sentence Checker: https://sentencechecker.com/ Free online spell and grammar checker, this is an open-source proofreading software which can help with getting your text right.

Take Charge and Get Results

I have found there are two kinds of people in the world: those who would like success and those who are serious about success. Think about it. Everyone *wants* success in their life; they want to make more money, have more time, have less stress and really make their mark in the world. The people who actually do it are the people who will not accept any alternatives.

For many people, it is easier to blame circumstance, adversity, their childhood, lack of status, job, boss, family, spouse, etc., for their results. For some, the source of blame is luck. "If only I were luckier," they cry again and again, always playing victim to some unseen force. Those who have massive success, however, have decided to take full control over their lives and to be personally responsible for their results. They recognize and learn from their errors and mistakes and revel in the glory of their wins and accomplishments.

The key to taking control of your destiny and your results is to become a person of responsibility. Meaning that you recognize in your life that you are responsible, and have always been responsible, for the outcome. In doing so, there is a tremendous amount of freedom and peace. Not only do you realize that in being responsible, you are in control, but you are no longer victim to circumstance, other people, or chance. You have the opportunity to create your results. Win or lose, it is completely up to you.

Napoleon Hill, author of *Think and Grow Rich*, ingeniously stated, "Every adversity, every failure and every headache carries with it the Seed of an equivalent or a greater Benefit." Accepting full responsibility for our results allows us to become creative, dynamic, and focused on exactly what we want, not what we *don't* want. We recognize success in our failures, learn from our mistakes, and move proactively on. The person who is personally responsible is solution-focused and empowered.

Consider this example: two people both start restaurants in the same town (Owner A & Owner B). They specialize in the same type of cuisine, have equally beneficial locations and the same amount of business/restaurant experience.

After 6 months of business, Owner A and Owner B find themselves at a crossroads. Their business has not been as successful as they had hoped, and both are facing dire financial situations. They contact you, a professional business consultant who specializes in assisting business owners in growing and developing their businesses into thriving enterprises.

Owner A spends most of the meeting complaining about the stingy customers, the lack of traffic, the vendors he uses, and the quality of his staff. You hear him openly criticize one of his waitstaff. You can feel the stress in the air and the staff seem frustrated and nervous. Owner A goes on and on about the tragedy of his business and tells you he plans to file for bankruptcy in two months if you don't help him. You ask Owner A for his proposed solution, and he puts it on you, asking if you can save his business. He begins complaining about your fees and is almost accusing in his tone and demeanour.

Owner B spends most of his time praising his staff and customers. The wait staff is friendly and smiling, and everyone is eager to be at the establishment. The owner tells you he recognized that, while he has a great establishment, he will require improvement to grow. He tells you he should have hired a marketing consultant in the beginning but thought he could do it on his own. He recognizes that to grow his business, he will have to bring more customers into the door and have their experience be so great they will want to come back as repeat customers. He shares his ideas with you and asks for your input, letting you know that he is committed to creating a great dining experience and a flourishing business. He also recognizes that your fees must indicate your value and the value you will provide to him. He is happy to see that you are proud of your work and feel deserving of your fees, as he knows this indicates your professionalism and experience.

After 12 months, who do you believe will still be in business, and who, as a business consultant, would you be eager to assist? Obviously, Owner B. Owner B realizes he has made some mistakes, and he has taken full responsibility for them. By doing so, he has recognized where he can improve and has asked for your assistance for guidance and direction, rather than seeing you as the lifesaver that will keep him from drowning.

Taking control of our results is a direct result of accepting responsibility. There is power in knowing what we achieve, or don't achieve, is a direct result of the actions we take. In this is there is freedom and the reality that we can truly achieve whatever it is we focus on. As Napoleon Hill said in *Think and Grow Rich*, "Anything the mind of a man can conceive and believe, he can achieve."

The choice is yours.

Make sure you have a Minimal Viable Product

It often amazes me how many new businesses want to start operations with an idea they think people want without ever once talking to a potential customer or doing any form of market research. Sometimes weeks and months go by with no success from sales and they begin to wonder why, trying to decipher the mind of their so-called target market only to fall flat on their face and ultimately send themselves out of business.

Even if you have a great idea, and I mean a real doozy, you still need to do some checking to see if there is actually a market for what you are trying to peddle. Your customers, your target market will quickly tell you what they think of your idea, and this can be very helpful in understanding the direction you should go.

When it comes to getting started, you want something that is simple, effective, and meets a demand of some sort. It does not have to be perfect from day one; in fact, it most likely will not be. It may take years of trials and modification to get the final product right, if ever, but you need to get going, and you need to be working towards continuous improvement in your products. Consumers demand change, and they are the best source of research and innovation you can have. This product needs to be easily brought to market and have value and meet a need. This is called your Minimum Viable Product or MVP.

Ash Maurya defines a Minimum Viable Product in the simplest way that I have heard:

"A Minimum Viable Product is the smallest thing you can build that delivers customer value (and as a bonus captures some of that value back)."

The reason you need to create a product you can sell as quickly as you can is you won't survive if you're not selling. Bringing home the bacon is paramount if you want to keep the lights on.

Sadly, many products that are brought to market have not been researched sufficiently beforehand and suffer the fate of so many potentially great ideas. Don't get me wrong, there are always some who make a really great product from day one and soar, but for many, the lack of good research and homework is, more often than not, a killing blow.

When you look at an MVP, you need to follow three simple rules.

1. Begin with something that is simple and can appeal to a small subset of the greater target market. Let it be the precursor to solving an even bigger problem.

2. Modify, improve, and develop the product as you go, collecting information from your clients, stakeholders, and general audience. Use this to fill the greater need, then the next need, and the next. Eventually, if you solve enough problems, you will solve the ultimate problem, and consumers will love you.

3. Always keep the goal in sight. What are you trying to achieve? What will your product or service solve? What have the customers said they want?

Elon Musk is one of the most inspirational people. He is not a person to sit around and complain about why things can't be done. I have followed his progress for years and listened to his ideas and philosophies learning what I can about the way he thinks and the way he plans. Sadly, I procrastinated buying Tesla shares in 2013 when I started my training company. I had money and was set for a great year. I had been really interested in his companies and ideas and so on Jan 2nd, 2013, shares in Tesla opened at US$35.00 each.

I thought to myself that I should buy some of them now as I could see his attitude was going to win over his failures. So you know what I did...I forgot about it! Days turned into months, which turned into years, and I never bought shares in Tesla. At the time of writing this, they are worth US$950.

Yes, the Life of a Procrastinator is such that there are so many things we wished we had done. Mind you, while Musk has no plans to list SpaceX anytime, I can assure you I stand at the ready.

When I look at how Elon Musk built his empire, there are very subtle points you can see happening. Look closely and see what they are.

Looking at Point One listed above, let's start a car company. Okay, not quite a small idea, but you will see the points soon. In 2006, in his "Master Plan, Part Deux", Musk wrote,

"I thought [Tesla's] chances of success were so low that I didn't want to risk anyone's funds in the beginning but my own."

His aim was not just to build cars. That was a means to an end, so to speak. He wanted to *"achieve a sustainable energy economy devoid of fossil fuels, the faster the better."* Fortunately, it took only a few years to become one of the fastest-selling electric car companies in the world.

Point Two is what Elon Musk does well: he modifies and improves constantly. He is always working on making things better. That's the engineer coming out in him, I'm sure.

He improved the battery life of his vehicles so that they travelled further. He helped to improve performance and created self-driving capability to reduce accidents. From car batteries to solar panels, Elon Musk has always focused on his goal of sustainable energy. That's what he is selling. Everything else is just the tools he uses to do it.

He isn't the greatest of communicators, as you can see from interviews and news reports. He seems, at times, awkward, yet this never stops him from expressing ideas to the public. Musk once said, "Let's get started today and see what's the biggest hole we can dig between now and Sunday afternoon, running 24 hours a day." Later that day, the cars were gone and there was a hole in the ground.

Thus, in December 2016 the Boring company was formed. Why? To reduce traffic congestion, travel times and pollution in Los Angeles. Once again, look back at why he does what he does. His product was selling the idea of a better world and for the most part he seems to be achieving it.

Point Three is a favourite. Musk is always willing to talk about his ideas, in fact he encourages people to use his technology and improve it. He captures imaginations because he is always talking about his vision, his purpose, his passion.

Can you contemplate what might have happened if Elon Musk built the tunnel between LAX to Culver City, then to Santa Monica, then to end in Westwood? A trip of 45 minutes would be reduced to 5. People would have laughed at him. Consider if he had built the massive Gigafactory to produce batteries. Most people laughed as he tried to compete with Phillips and other major brands. His journey would have stopped with an MVP that has no backbone and no viability. But it did not stop, thankfully.

He wanted us to come on the journey with him. I think that's why he funded Tesla himself when he started. It cost nothing for us to watch the journey, so we had nothing to lose. By letting us come along for the ride, we have bought into Elon Musk's dream. We have been sold on the Grand Prize. We have been won over by his version of an MVP, and now we want more.

So now, imagine you're on a journey to launch a new product. There are groups of customers who have signed up to be one of the first for the initial release of your product. You ask them all to do an online survey, which ends up showing some interesting results. There was evidence of purchases but nothing close to the number of people who initially signed up pre-release. Now, some would say this may be a real problem, but I do not look at it that way.

When you consider the results, it can be promising to think that there were people who purchased your product based on your initial vision. This is a win as it validates your initial target market prediction. Now you need to go out and speak to people find out what they are thinking and do some homework.

There are several things you need to ask to find out what is happening:

1. Ask them to explain to you what they first saw in the vision of the product you described to them. What caught their attention?
2. Is there anything about the product that makes it hard for them to catch the vision of what you are trying to sell?
3. Do they think there are competitors who have a better product?

4.   What do they think the competitors are doing better?

5.   Does the product you have released solve any of the problems they wanted solved from such a product?

Doing research will help you redefine the product or service you are releasing. It will give you a sense of purpose to fix those issues that have been raised. Hopefully, it will inspire you also to keep developing and creating. After all, these are the steps you need to take to reach your end goal, so don't forget that.

Finally, there are a few things you must always remember to focus on when developing a strong MVP. I know it sounds a bit cliché to say that a "strong" MVP means having a reasonably good product because people will not buy junk.

Remove all uncertainty. Look for the aspects of your product you know work and stick with them. Remove all possible situations designed to confuse or hinder the process of development. Don't waste money in the desperate hope things will get better. Stay focused on the objective. Avoid things that will take you off track and disrupt the creative and development process.

Be smart about decisions. There have been several times when I have had to ask myself, "Is it a good product?" "Is it really worth all the trouble to make it?" "Is this product able to generate a sustainable business model around?" Take time to consider all your options before venturing out on your first initial MVP. Sometimes, sitting back for a minute and contemplating the decisions you are going to have to make will help you avoid the wrong ones. It will give your brain time to catch up to your heart.

Be ready to move. Once you have developed your idea for the product or service, begin streamlining it and refining it some more. Ask yourself questions along the way, justify your answers with strong arguments, and get your friends to do the same. Constructive criticism is great for getting the real answer to a problem. Once you have some strong knowledge behind your product coupled with great research and findings, be ready to toss it all away and move in a different direction. Therefore, changes in direction during product or service development is so important to understand. Sometimes, these things creep up on you and change the entire perspective of what you're trying to achieve, so you must be ready for it.

Be willing to learn. Once you accept the fact that you do not know everything, you will find the world opens to such an extent that things become clearer and more defined. This is when the process of development and design improves and time to markets can often be reduced. Once you understand what to make or offer your customers because you have listened to the findings, you may not have to wait so long for your product to come to market. Then you simply have to make minor corrections along the way.

PART FOUR

2020 and Beyond

Well, what can I say about 2020? A year full of frustration, isolation, annoyance, and all-round exhaustion. That will be a year that will live in the memories of many for a long time.

I was surprised when I looked back at how much I had actually achieved, even under strict isolation rules. So, I wanted to share some final words on a couple of things I have learned, developed, taught, and followed throughout the year.

This book is most likely my biggest joy to come out of 2020. I have wanted to write a book for so long and see my name on its cover. Writing this is a bucket list event for me. I never intended to write a book for the fame or glory, merely to say I have done it. The feeling of being able to search for the title and see something I created available to everyone is a real treat for me.

It took a lot of nights where I'd get up after everyone else had gone to bed, sit alone in the dark in front of my computer, and tap away at the keyboard. I seemed to be able to get my thoughts out much simpler when there were no distractions. Normally, I have no issues with noise around me, but for this project, the quieter, the better.

Some people asked me what the point was if you did not want to make money from it. I told them I never said I did not want to make money; however, that was not my driving force for it. It was a lifelong personal goal—something I wanted to achieve for myself—something I could reflect on and say, you know what, I did that.

I also began developing my own business a lot more. I have spent a lot of time planning and strategizing the hows and whys of what I am doing. I think my personal self-efficacy has helped me understand what I can and can't do, which has led me to become more focused on achieving what I know I can achieve. The areas I need help with, well, I have asked for it.

It's a big step for me to ask for help now, one that I think was due. I have felt I am back where I started from in 2013, and now, I can focus on achieving some real growth for myself, my family, and my business.

I also made a commitment to myself. It's a big one, but I think it will help me focus my attention on what I want to achieve. I have decided not to work for anyone again. I want to work for myself. I want the freedom it brings in being your own boss, but I also want the flexibility to pursue ideas, try things, and take calculated risks. In essence, I want some adventure that I can control.

A few friends have said it's a brave thing to do, but I have been doing it on and off for a long time but never really committed to it. It always seemed to be an element of my life that was in the background. I helped many people achieve their dreams at the expense of my own, and 2020 showed me that with patience and the right planning, I can achieve my own goals and objectives.

Yes, I know it is a tall order, and yes, I know some of you are saying that your income will be very precarious, but I actually think I will be ok. I have some businesses I work "with" at present, and I have been able to be very upfront about my plans with them. They have respected my decisions and have wanted to continue the relationship, which is great. It gives me the flexibility to do what I need and yet still have some income from helping others. I know it will be a little up and down, but with my goals firmly focused, I am confident that I can make things happen.

Oh, don't forget to have fun. Fun can come in any form and often out of the blue. It is a vital part of your journey, and if you don't take time to enjoy things, then life could become very mundane and depressing. I have tried to see the fun in what I am doing, as I think it is important not to lose sight of what I am trying to do.

Side note: I had the opportunity to sit in on a session entitled "Digital Immigrants Raising Digital Natives: Parenting in an Uncharted E-World" by Dr Timothy Rarick, who is a Professor of Marriage & Family Studies at BYU-Idaho. His insights into how digital technology affects our youth were excellent, and I found a lot of similarities in what we have mentioned in this book.

Distractions that take us away from our goals can be digital, too. I mean, who hasn't found their way onto YouTube or Facebook in the middle of the day when working and realised 3 hours later that you did not achieve what you wanted?

"It is named the "Web" for good reason."

David Foster Wallace

I tell you this because, during the session, I noticed something. On the desk to the right of Dr Rarick was what looked like a ceramic Pig. I could not for the life of me get it out of my mind, so I asked him at the end, "What is with the pig?" His reply was funny as he did not know what I was talking about. I had to explain to him (to the amusement of those still on the call) to look around, and behind him, I was referring to the pig on the bench. He laughed and picked it up and said he thought it was some bizarre Australian slang term I was using. I feel this has now spawned a new term in the world of digital media; I forever dub the unique item in the background of a video conference call that you cannot stop looking at as "The Pig on the Bench".

Having fun is such an important part of starting a business or creating a new product or service. If you are not enjoying it, then why are you doing it?

Anyway, lastly is that I have reset a goal of being financially independent by the time I am 50. I have two years to make it happen. This does not mean I want to be rich and never have to work again, but rather, I want to be in a financial position to have a choice. I do not want to be locked down to a life of forced work simply to pay the bills. Yes, having a bank full of money would be nice, but I would rather have an income stream, or several that are working for me continually, giving me the flexibility to choose what I want to do.

It's a tall order, I know, but I figured if I don't have any goals set, then what am I aiming for? I mean, after all, this is what I teach people, so it's about time I stop procrastinating about it.

We Made It

So, here we are. I have finally finished the book I have been wanting to write for so long. I must say, I am feeling a little proud (but also a bit exhausted).

"Sometimes exhaustion is not a result of too much time spent on something, but of knowing that in its place, no time is spent on something else."

Joyce Rachelle

It was a big job, but I have had lots of time at home due to the Coronavirus. It was only right that I used this extra time to finish writing the book I started so long ago.

I wanted to let you all know that procrastination can drag you backwards in many aspects of business life. If there is one thing I have learnt along this journey, it is that saying, "I will do it tomorrow" just never seems to work.

We all need to achieve something every day. It does not matter if it is big or small, but achieve something. Do not let a day go by as a business owner where you do not achieve something. Fill your life with purpose and ambition and you will feel the same way I feel now (maybe not so exhausted, though).

My last piece of wisdom is simple. There really is no right or wrong way to do things. If it works for you and you achieve the desired results you want, then that's how you do it. Your business or ideas are yours, and do not let anyone take them from you. Work hard, strive for happiness, and have fun doing it.

OK, you can go now.

Oh, one last thing. If you enjoyed the read and think I'm deserving, please consider leaving a review on Amazon. It would mean a lot to me.

RESOURCES

Articles

- 3 Ways Focus Will Help You Succeed in Life by Bryan Oliver

- 7 Reasons to Join a Mastermind Group by Stephanie Burns

- 8 Ways to Develop Long-Term Focus and Achieve Success by Adam Toren

- Gary Vee: 'Don't Be Worried About Content Fatigue, Nobody's Going to See It All by Farzanah Farveen

- How to Critically Assess Your Personal Strengths and Weaknesses by Adam Sicinski

- Improving Your Business Knowledge by Richard Stewart

- The Manager's Guide to Understanding Strategy: Getting Started by Art Petty

- How to Pick your Battles : Four Key Questions To Ask by Sally Percy

- Four questions to ask yourself before picking a battle by WORKOPOLIS,

- **14 Famous Business Pivots** by Jason Nazar of Forbes.com

- What Is Passive Income? By Gayle Sato

- Books
- The 21 Irrefutable Laws of Leadership: Follow Them and People Will Follow You by John C. Maxwell
- The Art of War by Sun Tzu
- How to Win Friends and Influence People by Dale Carnegie
- Influence: The Psychology of Persuasion by Robert Cialdini
- Outliers: The Story of Success by Malcolm Gladwell
- Start with Why: How Great Leaders Inspire Everyone to Take Action by Simon Sinek
- The Richest Man in Babylon by George S. Clason
- Seven Habits of Highly Effective People Stephen R. Covey
- Strengths Finder 2.0 by Tom Rath
- Think and Grow Rich by Napoleon Hill
- The Psychology of Self-Esteem by Nathaniel L. Branden
- Wealth of Words by Amit Kalantri
- The Art of War by Sun Tzu

Icons created by

- Jozef Mikulcik –
  https://pixabay.com/users/jozefm8-10215106/

Cartoons by

- Gadtoons - https://www.fiverr.com/gadtoons
- YSFworks - https://www.fiverr.com/ysfworks

ABOUT THE AUTHOR

Prof. Gaven Ferguson does not see himself as a guru. He is a regular guy who spends his life teaching and helping others, often to the detriment of his own dreams. He is passionate and committed to making a difference. He finds joy in making others happy and seeing people succeed in business and in their pursuits. He has tried to inspire people in his talks, workshops, and training programs.

He loves to travel, exploring places that are off the beaten track, and when not building models, playing D&D with his friends (Yes, I know, but let it go), gardening, or writing, his passions and commitments are as the Global President of the World Association of Master Chefs, Adjunct Professor of UCIS University in Malaysia, Owner and Managing Director of the Hospitality & Tourism Industry Accreditation Program (HATIA), and RLP Assess Pty Ltd, and is a consultant to anyone who needs him.

He holds a Master's in Marketing Management and a Degree in Business Commerce from Griffith University and at least eight other Graduate Diplomas and Diplomas, all related to the business world.

Gaven has been married to his wife for 30 years and has two beautiful daughters who inspire him to aim for the sky and never question his weird and often crazy approach to life. His wife, on the other hand, questions him constantly, but that is what he loves about her.

Other Books By Pro. Gaven Ferguson

- The Wisest Man in Giza: Lessons from the Business Pyramid, Released 2025 – Amazon

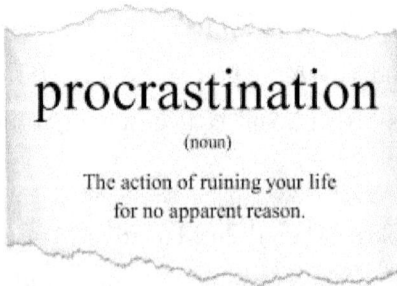

procrastination

(noun)

The action of ruining your life
for no apparent reason.

www.ingramcontent.com/pod-product-compliance
Lightning Source LLC
La Vergne TN
LVHW051624080426
835511LV00016B/2154